Greger Von der Muhl

76

D0547263

THE LIBER
THEORY OF JUSTICE

THE LIBERAL
THEORY OF JUSTICE

A Critical Examination
of the Principal Doctrines in
A Theory of Justice by John Rawls

BY

BRIAN BARRY

CLARENDON PRESS   OXFORD

Oxford University Press, Ely House, London W.1

GLASGOW NEW YORK TORONTO MELBOURNE WELLINGTON
CAPE TOWN IBADAN NAIROBI DAR ES SALAAM LUSAKA ADDIS ABABA
DELHI BOMBAY CALCUTTA MADRAS KARACHI LAHORE DACCA
KUALA LUMPUR SINGAPORE HONG KONG TOKYO

CASEBOUND ISBN o 19 824509 2
PAPERBACK ISBN o 19 875032 3

© OXFORD UNIVERSITY PRESS 1973

Excerpts from *A Theory of Justice* by John Rawls are printed
by permission of the Clarendon Press, Oxford and the
Belknap Press of Harvard University Press. Copyright ©
1971 by the President and Fellows of Harvard College.

*All rights reserved. No part of this publication may be reproduced,
stored in a retrieval system, or transmitted, in any form or by any means,
electronic, mechanical, photocopying, recording or otherwise, without
the prior permission of Oxford University Press.*

First published 1973
Reprinted (with corrections) 1975

TYPESETTING BY LINOCOMP LIMITED,
CHURCH STREET, MARCHAM, BERKS.

PRINTED IN GREAT BRITAIN BY
WILLIAM CLOWES & SONS, LIMITED
LONDON, BECCLES AND COLCHESTER

ACKNOWLEDGEMENTS

This book was written (among other things) while I was the only passenger on a four-month round trip from Piraeus to Mombasa and back on a Greek freighter, the *Hellenic Halcyon*, in the summer of 1972. It is a pleasure to thank the officers and crew, and especially Captain Anastasios Moumoulidis, for providing the ideal working environment as well as a very pleasant and interesting voyage. The whole draft has been read by Professor H. L. A. Hart and John Flemming, and a part by David Soskice. I have benefited greatly from their detailed comments. My wife Joanna not only mowed the grass and paid the bills in my absence but also typed out the contents of the airmail envelopes posted from various African ports. An article drawn from material in Chapters 3 and 11 has been published in *Political Theory* and a variant of Chapter 7 in *Philosophy and Public Policy*. I should mention that it was an invitation from the Editor of the latter journal to write something about *A Theory of Justice*, and my acceptance of his invitation, which resulted in the production of the present book, since I found, when I got down to it, that it was impossible to provide a serious overall judgement within the limits of an article. The final acknowledgement must go to Professor Rawls, who made this book possible not only by writing *A Theory of Justice* but by generously giving permission for me to quote from it here.

Nuffield College,   December 1972
Oxford.

CONTENTS

APOLOGIA

IT is not usually considered necessary to justify the writing of a short book (this is about 70,000 words) about a long one (*A Theory of Justice* contains some 280,000 words). Indeed, there are many long commentaries on short books. What is liable to make the present enterprise appear eccentric by contemporary standards—though not those of earlier times—is that the book to which I here address myself was published only recently. I am, in effect, anticipating the winnowing work of time in assuming, and acting on the assumption, that *A Theory of Justice* is a work of major importance and one which will repay the careful attention which I have here tried to devote to it. I do believe this to be so, and all the reviews which I have seen concur in signalling *A Theory of Justice* as a work of great significance for moral and political philosophy. The conclusion I draw from this is that a brief review is of little more value than would be a brief review of Hobbes's *Leviathan.* If *A Theory of Justice* is a major work it should be treated as one expects a major work to be treated: that is to say, discussed with some pretence to thoroughness, at least in relation to its central tenets.

The general drift of this book, as the reader will discover, is that Rawls's 'theory of justice' does not work and that many of of his individual arguments are unsound. But I should be extremely mortified if anything I say in it should lead anyone to believe that *A Theory of Justice* is worthy of anything less than prolonged and intensive study. I may indeed hope that my decision to write a commentary at this length ought to be a sufficient indication of my ideas about the book's value. It is, quite simply, a work that anyone in future who proposes to deal with any of the topics it touches must first come to terms with if he expects the scholarly community to take him seriously.

I fear that what I have written will at some points displease and perhaps even offend Professor Rawls, for whose single-minded dedication to developing his ideas I have the greatest respect. But I take comfort from his own statement that 'being first virtues of human activities, truth and justice are uncompromising' (page 4) and I hope that my lapses from the literary virtues of tact and good taste will be at least partly mitigated in the light of it.

'A theory', writes Rawls, 'however elegant and economical must be rejected or revised if it is untrue.' (Page 3.) But if there is no substitute for truth in theories, there is an important additional criterion for books: that they should express clearly and coherently a distinct point of view and thus provoke thought. On this criterion Rawls succeeds triumphantly. Rawls, with his 'clear and distinct ideas', gives us something to get our teeth into, unlike the numerous practitioners of 'safety first' with their 'it may be thought thats' and 'on the one hand and on the other hands'. Whether, having chewed, we swallow or not, we can truly say with Old Father William that

> the muscular strength, which it gave to my jaw,
> Has lasted the rest of my life.

I

INTRODUCTION

'THIS is a long book, not only in pages', writes the author (page viii). This is so. It weighs in at over a quarter of a million words—about equivalent to three books of the average length of modern books devoted purely to analysis and argument. It is not, as Rawls says, merely that there are a lot of words. The book is not padded out with laborious discussions of what this or that Great Man said. There is, it is true, a certain amount of redundancy, with similar arguments coming round several times in different places. But this in fact is an additional source of difficulty, because the reader has to decide whether he is getting the same argument expressed slightly differently or a slightly different argument that looks much the same. What makes it long in every sense is that from the first page to the last it is simply crammed with arguments. This is literally true. In the final paragraph (on page 587) we find Rawls still firing arguments at us in a last attempt to remove any lingering doubts we may still be harbouring. 'Finally, we may remind ourselves that the hypothetical nature of the original position invites the question: why should we take any interest in it, moral or otherwise? Recall the answer . . .' and then bang, bang, bang for the last time.

As well as length, density and partial repetition, another thing that makes the book a hard one to read is the constant need of referring backwards and forwards, and the difficulty sometimes of knowing where one is going or why. In the intro-duction to the last of the three Parts into which the book is divided the author writes: 'Sometimes in this part the overall direction of the exposition may seem less clear, and the transi-tion from one topic to another more abrupt.' (Page 395.) 'A mighty maze! but not without a plan', says the author; but, like the Author whom Pope advised us against presuming to scan, he is open to the complaint that it is sometimes hard to see what the plan is. Some of the later sections (there are eighty-seven altogether, indicated here as in Rawls's text by a §) read rather like extended notes to earlier sections which could not conveniently be fitted in at the earlier place without breaking the thread of the argument. It might have been better for these to be gathered at the end as a series of notes to the main text.

There are further difficulties, which may be attributed to the book's unusually long gestation period. Before appearing in their present setting many of the central points in Rawls's theory of justice have been published in a series of articles stretching back to 'Justice as Fairness' in 1958,[1] and the book has in that time gone through two or three earlier drafts which have had a private circulation in typescript. Rawls says in his Preface (pages x–xii) that he has attempted to deal with all the criticisms, published and unpublished, that have come to his notice during this gestation period. But he does not usually mention these criticisms explicitly and say that a certain point he is making was provoked by a certain criticism. This again makes for difficulties. When reading the book I found at times that the only way to grasp the purport of a paragraph was to recall what objection it was a reply to, and I do not much doubt that in other cases where I was lost this was due to the fact that I had not seen the relevant objection.

Another problem arising from the long gestation period is that Rawls seems to have altered his views subtly during the period. Where originally the emphasis was on morality as a system of mutual self-defence, rather like a refined version of Hobbes's 'natural law',[2] the emphasis now rests on the desire to act justly being a central aspect of human development, a natural (and reflectively supported) extension of love for particular people and loyalty to particular associations. The desire to be just and to co-operate in the maintenance of a just society

---

1. 'Justice as Fairness', *Philosophical Review*, lxvii (1958), 164–94. Reprinted in P. Laslett and W. G. Runciman (eds.), *Philosophy, Politics and Society*, Second Series (Oxford: Basil Blackwell, 1962).

2. Or perhaps even more precisely Hart's 'minimum content of natural law'. See Chapter IX of H. L. A. Hart, *The Concept of Law* (Oxford: Clarendon Press, 1961).

is something that a man cannot frustrate except at the cost of stunting his moral nature, which is the most important part of himself. This change of viewpoint is reflected in the style. The terse prose of 'Justice as Fairness' gives way to an earnest eloquence which at times, in the last third of the book, approaches the rhapsodic.

This change in Rawls's outlook does not on the whole create problems for the book considered in itself. There is, I think, at one point an incoherence in the argument that may plausibly be attributed to the shift, but that is all. (I shall mention it in due course.) It is more serious in relation to the book's reception. The early reviews that I have seen treat the book as if it were simply a reprint of the already published articles plus some linking material, and it may well be that others who know the articles will, on the basis of the same notion, not think it worth reading the book. This would be a mistake. The new material is extensive and important. Even more to the point, it has the effect of changing the balance of the book, giving it a more Kantian slant than one would previously have expected.

The index gives a good picture of the book's concerns.[3] In terms of authors, Kant and Sidgwick lead with sixteen lines apiece, plus another sixteen on the 'Kantian interpretation of justice as fairness'. J. S. Mill follows with eleven lines and then comes Bentham with seven. Hume and Aristotle get five lines apiece, though there are also seventeen lines on the 'Aristotelian principle', which will be discussed later. No other author rates more than three lines, and these are mostly footnote references.

Painting with broad strokes, we might represent Rawls as being to Kant as Sidgwick was to Hume and Bentham. Sidgwick turned the offhand references of Hume and Bentham to 'utility' into a fully elaborated and carefully applied system. Similarly, Rawls may be conceived as putting into a rigorous and fully developed form the ideas of the utilitarians' main rivals, the

---

3. No praise is too high for the clarity and comprehensiveness of the index, which is truly a model of what an index should be for a book of this kind. I well know how many hours of taxing labour must have gone into creating such an index. Because of the need to collect together the things said in different parts of the book on the same topic the index is peculiarly vital, and this one goes as far towards obviating the difficulties caused by the book's organization as any could do.

men Rawls himself calls the 'contract theorists'.[4] In particular, from his present standpoint, the figure of Kant is central. Of great interest here is a long footnote about Kant, the first part of which runs as follows. 'To be avoided at all costs is the idea that Kant's doctrine simply provides the general, or formal, elements for a utilitarian (or indeed for any other) theory. . . .[5] One must not lose sight of the full scope of his view, one must take the later works into consideration.' (Page 251.) It is clear from the works he goes on to cite and from the book itself that he intends to refer here to Kant as a social and political theorist and also to Kant as a moral psychologist.

The comparison of Rawls with Sidgwick is, I think, illuminating. Both *A Theory of Justice* and *The Methods of Ethics*,[6] which appeared just two years short of a century before it, are comprehensive and systematic statements of a thoroughgoing liberal position; and both, it might be added, appear at a time when liberalism is becoming unfashionable, dismissed in smart circles as shallow compared with the deep (not to say unfathomable) truths of Hegel or a Hegelianized Marx.

I can think of no better way to introduce this discussion of *A Theory of Justice* than by pursuing the comparison with *The Methods of Ethics* at a more detailed level. For although Rawls spends a good deal of time trying to show that Sidgwick's utilitarianism should be rejected, this careful attention itself reflects a striking similarity in aims and approaches. One might say that it is just because of their closeness that Rawls can engage with Sidgwick, rather in the same way that the bitterest controversies often occur between political factions close together on the political spectrum. I have selected five points for comparison, which I shall take in order. They are as follows: (1) the two authors share a common conception of the general nature of the enterprise; (2) both reject 'intuitionism', though

4. Their main rivals, that is, apart from 'common sense' or 'intuitionist' theorists. As I point out below, both Sidgwick and Rawls regard 'common sense' morality as something that must be come to terms with but must if possible be transcended by a comprehensive doctrine from which our most confident 'common-sense' judgements can be derived.

5. The omitted sentence runs: 'See, for example, R. M. Hare, *Freedom and Reason* (Oxford: Clarendon Press, 1963), pp. 123 f.' I shall discuss the relation between the theories of Rawls and Hare below.

6. H. Sidgwick, *The Methods of Ethics*. First edition 1874; seventh edition 1907 (London: Macmillan, reissued 1962).

what they mean by it is slightly different; (3) both regard utilitarianism as a moral theory of major significance, though one accepts and the other rejects it; (4) Sidgwick deals with three 'methods' of ethics, and his third (in addition to intuitionism and utilitarianism) is egoism, which Rawls dismisses relatively briefly; (5) Rawls, however, also has three approaches which are taken seriously, and adds to intuitionism and utilitarianism his own 'contract theory of justice'.

(1) *The nature of the enterprise.* For Sidgwick the 'morality of common sense' is an indispensable touchstone of any ethical theory. To be acceptable a theory must not have practical implications that run counter to our firmest common-sense convictions about right and wrong. But if a theory satisfies this criterion and has other advantages of generality and plausibility we may follow the theory and reject our less certain 'common-sense' judgements where the implications of the theory are different. Rawls has much the same conception of the ground rules of ethical argument. He follows Sidgwick precisely in maintaining that any general theory must, if it is to be accepted, accommodate the more confident of our 'common-sense' judgements, though we may elsewhere abandon 'common sense' in favour of the deductions from the theory. The final stage, in which we have modified our general theory so that its implications will not offend the 'common-sense' judgements we feel we must adhere to, and reconciled ourselves to bringing the rest of our detailed judgements into line with the implications of the theory, Rawls describes as 'reflective equilibrium'. (See pages 19–21.) This is surely a concept that Sidgwick could have acknowledged as a way of characterizing his own aim. Where the two writers differ is not in the way they see the problem but in the answer they give.

(2) *Intuitionism.* Sidgwick and Rawls both treat something they call 'intuitionism' as the closest philosophically-respectable approximation to 'common sense' and both believe that it can be transcended by something more comprehensive and rigorous. What they mean by 'intuitionism' is, however, rather different. For Sidgwick the 'intuitionist method' consists in starting with a ragbag of unconnected low-level maxims of conduct and trying to fit them together into a consistent whole. Rawls's 'intuitionism' operates at a higher level. For him the mark of

an 'intuitionist' is that he believes in a plurality of 'ultimate values' which cannot be unequivocally ranked but have to be traded-off against one another in judging actions, institutions etc. Rawls says that this view might be called 'pluralism', and this would certainly seem to me a happier form of appellation. Sidgwick, after all, believed that utilitarianism could only be founded upon one fundamental intuition and there does not seem to be anything intrinsically more intuitive about two or three fundamental intuitions than about one.[7]

Sidgwick concluded, after his examination of intuitionism, as he defined it, that it was irremediably involved in inconsistency. Rawls, however, suggests that his pluralistic intuitionism has 'nothing intrinsically irrational' about it. 'Indeed,' he says, 'it may be true. . . . The only way therefore to dispute intuitionism is to set forth the recognizably ethical criteria that account for the weights which, in our considered judgments, we think appropriate to give to the plurality of principles. A refutation of intuitionism consists in presenting the sort of constructive criteria that are said not to exist.' (Page 39.) Rawls, however, is not a monist. He does not have one single principle comparable to the utilitarian formula. But his pluralism does not commit him to trading off principles against one another and it is for that reason that he thinks of himself as having overcome 'intuitionism'. Although he has more than one principle, he gives priority rules for the principles. Thus if there are two principles one of them only comes into play to break ties if two or more alternatives are equally good on the basis of the other principle, which is above it in the hierarchy. I shall suggest later, however, that this kind of relationship among independent principles is a highly peculiar one with curious implications.

---

7. With some embarrassment I have to mention here that I am cited as one of three 'intuitionists', the others being Nicholas Rescher and Richard Brandt, It may be that I can claim the priority for having tricked out the basic idea of pluralism in the trappings of indifference curve analysis, in which case the credit goes to the Oxford PPE School, now sadly dismembered. (Rawls uses this apparatus to explain 'intuitionism' on pages 37–9.) But the idea itself is surely of longer and more august parentage (if I may say so with due respect to Professors Rescher and Brandt) than Rawls's citation implies. My own confidence in the notion, anyway, was sustained by the belief that it could be found in Sir Isaiah Berlin's *Two Concepts of Liberty* (Oxford: Clarendon Press, 1958) and H. L. A. Hart's views on the justification of punishment (see *Punishment and Responsibility* (Oxford: Clarendon Press, 1968)).

(3) *Utilitarianism.* Sidgwick argues that utilitarianism is a coherent and workable theory which fits our common-sense judgements at the crucial points and whose other implications can reasonably be accepted, even when they appear to be in conflict with 'common sense'. Rawls casts doubt on the possibility of applying utilitarianism, in particular because he denies that quantities of pleasure can be used as a common measure for the purpose of aggregating the happiness of different people. He also argues that its implications do not jibe with the judgements of common sense that we are most sure about, so that in any case it should be rejected. Within the framework of his own analysis he argues further that utilitarianism would not be a rational choice of principle in the 'original position'. I shall discuss this in its proper place below. The second point, that utilitarianism has (or may have) implications that are repugnant is, I think, quite widely accepted nowadays in that many people would accept, independently of Rawls's arguments, that some kind of distributive considerations have to be introduced as a constraint or a competing factor on the maximization of aggregate utility. If this is so, one might suggest that Rawls, in taking utilitarianism as the main rival to his own account, is flogging an almost dead stalking-horse. The first point, about the difficulty of applying utilitarianism, clearly has some force. But I shall argue later that Rawls's attempt to define principles so as to exclude any reference to pleasure, happiness, or anything subjective, leads to results more unpalatable than even a crude use of such concepts could give rise to.

(4) *Egoism.* Sidgwick takes the view that it is as rational to seek to maximize one's own happiness as to seek to maximize the sum of human happiness, though difficult to think of any plausible grounds for anything in between. He treats egoism at length, partly as a preparation for the discussion of utilitarianism but also as a 'method of ethics' in its own right. Rawls is a good deal more curt with egoism, dismissing it both as a rational aim and as a conceivable moral theory. The argument on the first head is that nobody who thinks about it seriously can want to be an egoist: 'acting justly is something we want to do as free and equal rational beings' (page 572). Egoists, Rawls suggests, would not be able to engage in relations of genuine friendship since they would be incapable of making

sacrifices for one another. And although they could be angry or annoyed at one another they would necessarily be unable to be indignant or resentful, because these reactions presuppose certain moral commitments. 'One may say, then, that a person who lacks a sense of justice, and who would never act as justice requires except as self-interest and expediency prompt, not only is without ties of friendship, affection, and mutual trust, but is incapable of experiencing resentment and indignation. . . . [He] lacks certain fundamental attitudes and capacities included under the notion of humanity.' (Page 488.)

As I understand it, all this is supposed to be assertable from within the 'thin theory of the good', which means that it should not require any substantive ideal of human character in order to be convincing. (The 'thin theory of the good' will be discussed in detail in Chapter 3.) This claim may not seem very plausible. But for the present purpose this does not matter too much because in any case Rawls argues that egoism, whether or not it is a rational aim for an individual, lacks the necessary requirements for being a moral theory. This depends on a more 'tough-minded' line of thought than the other, and (as we would expect from the development of Rawls's outlook) belongs to an earlier stratum of the theory. It is to be found near the beginning of the book whereas the more 'tender-minded', more Kantian, idea is to be found towards the end. What Rawls suggests, like many contract theorists and many others who are not,[8] is that morality is, at the minimum, a game of mutual informal coercion in which each person finds an advantage in helping to maintain the institution even if it would sometimes pay him to be a 'free rider' and break the rules. Thus, Rawls says that

although a society is a cooperative venture for mutual advantage, it is typically marked by a conflict as well as an identity of interests. . . . Thus principles are needed for choosing among the various social arrangements which determine [the] division of advantages and for underwriting an agreement on the proper distributive shares. These requirements define the role of justice. (Page 126.)

Rawls then argues that egoism fails to satisfy these requirements and sums up by saying that

8. For a recent example, see G. Warnock, *The Object of Morality* (London: Methuen and Co., 1971).

although egoism is logically consistent and in this sense not irrational, it is incompatible with what we intuitively regard as the moral point of view. The significance of egoism philosophically is not as an alternative conception of right but as a challenge to any such conception. (Page 136.)

(5) *Rawls's principles of justice.* As we have seen, Rawls rejects utilitarianism as an adequate general account of morality. But he has a general account to offer himself of the concept which he treats as the central concept of 'right', the concept of justice. The main purpose of the present book is to examine the way in which Rawls derives his principles of justice, and to look at their implications, so it would be absurd to anticipate that discussion here. But it will be helpful at least to state here what Rawls's principles of justice are. In their final form they run as follows:

First Principle. Each person is to have an equal right to the most extensive total system of equal basic liberties compatible with a similar system of liberty for all.
Second Principle. Social and economic inequalities are to be arranged so that they are both: (a) to the greatest benefit of the least advantaged, consistent with the just savings principle, and (b) attached to offices and positions open to all under the conditions of fair equality of opportunity. (Page 302.)

Merely to state the two principles, however, is to give only half the story and that, perhaps, the less important half. It is at this point that the change in emphasis since 'Justice as Fairness' becomes most dramatic. For Rawls also has rules for priority between the two principles and between the two parts of the second principle, and these radically affect the whole thrust of the theory. We have to add, then, that the first principle has absolute priority over the second (provided certain socio-economic conditions are fulfilled) and the second part of the second principle has absolute priority over the first part. Exactly what 'absolute priority' signifies here is something that will be discussed in some detail later.

2

THE ORIGINAL POSITION

RAWLS does not simply suggest that the two principles of justice square with 'common-sense' notions at the essential points while providing determinate and acceptable guidance elsewhere. He maintains that they are the principles that would be chosen by rational actors in an 'original position' where they did not know certain things about themselves. This *is* in fact the conception of 'justice as fairness': the idea that substantive regulative principles (principles of justice) can be derived from the consideration of a situation in which certain possibilities of pursuing self-interest by espousing one principle rather than another have been removed (conditions of fairness). In this chapter I shall examine what Rawls has to say about the 'original position' and discuss the conditions which he imposes on it.

The conditions of the 'original position' can be divided into two kinds: those which concern knowledge and those which concern motivation. The limits on knowledge, summarily stated, are that the actors do not know their social position, their particular talents or bents, or their 'conception of the good', which includes such things as their particular sources of pleasure, their ambitions, and their religion or other beliefs. As a further refinement, to deal with certain problems with the 'just savings rate', Rawls adds that they do not know what stage of economic development their society has reached. The limitations on knowledge Rawls refers to as a 'veil of ignorance'. The motivational postulates are first that the actors in the original position are rational and secondly that they are not altruistic. More precisely, the second condition means that each of them wishes to further his own 'conception of the good', though he does not—under the limitations of knowledge—know what content this conception will have. A man's 'conception of the good' may include in it the welfare of certain other people for whom he feels affection or special responsibility. But, for the purpose of the original position, it does not include a substantive sense of justice. That is to say, a man cannot, in the original position, take as his end the idea that everyone's welfare should be increased as much as possible, or say that he would like a certain distribution of goods or utilities for its own sake.

The relation between this 'original position' and the two principles of justice is held by Rawls to be, quite precisely, a deductive one. But it is important to understand what is claimed to be deducible and what is not. Thus, Rawls does not say that he can give a deductive proof of the proposition that whatever principles would be chosen in a suitably characterized original position are principles of justice. This part of the argument depends on the plausibility of the idea that the 'conditions of justice' are conditions of partial co-operation and partial conflict and the assertion that the conception of an 'original position' captures these features of the 'conditions of justice' while excluding irrelevancies. The claim to have established a deductive relationship applies to only one link in the chain: from an original position characterized in one particular way to the two principles of justice and the priority relationships among the principles and their parts. The claim can be put in a hypothetical form as follows: if the principles of justice are those principles which would be chosen in an original position characterized as Rawls characterizes it, then the 'two principles' are the principles of justice. 'We should strive for a kind of moral geometry with all the rigor which this term connotes.' (Page 121.) But, as with the axioms of geometry, the postulated conditions of the original position have to be accepted first. They cannot themselves be proved within the system. 'There are indefinitely many variations of the initial situation and therefore no doubt indefinitely many theorems of moral geometry.' (Page 126.) How then do we decide on a particular set of postulates to define the original position? The same reason for thinking that principles chosen in an original position would be principles of justice will guide us to a general conception of the postulates required. Beyond that, Rawls says frankly, we fiddle about with the conditions of the original position until they produce the deductions that we want to get out. At a minimum, that is to say, we have to keep adjusting them so that the principles deduced from them do not conflict with our unshakable 'common-sense' convictions of right and wrong.

In 'Justice as Fairness', Rawls gave the impression that he saw his most important distinctive contribution as lying in the conception of choice from behind a 'veil of ignorance' (though he did not yet call it that). Here he is willing, almost anxious, to point out that it is really no more than a dramatic way of setting out the conditions for impartial judgement. I would maintain indeed that there is not a great deal of practical difference between invoking Rawls's 'veil of ignorance' and simply demanding that an 'ideal observer' should behave impartially, or saying that people's moral judgements are more likely to be unprejudiced if their own interests are not at stake in the matter under decision. If we compare the machinery of the 'veil of ignorance' with the limitations imposed by R. M. Hare on the possible form and content of moral principles, we can, I think, go further and speak of an effective identity. For Hare's limitations on principles—no proper names or other specially identifying terms and so on—are designed to achieve precisely the same effect as Rawls's 'veil of ignorance'.

It is indeed interesting to note how close are the parallels between *A Theory of Justice* and *Freedom and Reason*. Rawls and Hare deduce moral principles from constrained self-interest and both do it in a similar way. Moreover, Hare's apparatus of 'interests' and 'ideals' has a basic resemblance to Rawls's 'primary goods' and their relation to the 'full theory of the good'. It is true that Hare finishes up by deriving the two principles of utilitarianism and equal distribution of want-satisfaction in some vaguely pluralistic relationship, whereas Rawls deduces a principle of maximizing the wealth and power of the worst-off. But these alternatives are not very far apart even on their face, and we have then to add these two points: (a) Hare is so vague about the trade-off relationship that, given what can be guessed of his political leanings, he might well accept something on Rawls's lines, and (b) Rawls sometimes suggests that his two principles with their priority relations are a rough-and-ready way of giving a version of the maximization/equalization mix that is acceptable and reduces to a minimum the amount of room for discrepant interpretations. In any case, any divergence at this stage after getting so close to the end of the road together is of relatively little significance. In spite of this, their recognition of one another's work in their books is like 'the curious incident of the dog in the night': Rawls gives Hare four (minor and uncomplimentary) footnote references, one of which has already been quoted, while *Freedom and Reason* does not mention 'Justice as Fairness', published five years before it. The explanation is not a sinister one. The history of invention is remarkably full of cases of independent discovery by two or more men of the same thing. This instance, however, has the ironic twist that the two inventors did not recognize that it was, by and large, the same thing.

It should, however, be added that Hare has recently argued explicitly that a theory of Rawls's kind (which he calls a 'rational contractor' theory) is 'practically equivalent' to his own type of theory (which he calls a 'universal prescriptive' theory).

Impartiality is guaranteed by the fact that my prescription has to apply in all cases resembling this one in their universal properties; since these will include cases (hypothetical or actual) in which I myself play the roles of each of the other parties affected, I am put by this theory in exactly the same position as the rational contractors.[1]

The 'veil of ignorance' by itself, then, is not what is distinctive about Rawls's approach. It is compatible with any view of morality which insists on the central role of impartiality. For example, W. G. Runciman, in his book *Relative Deprivation and Social Justice*,[2] borrows Rawls's notion of an original position simply as a way of asking what principles of distribution it would be reasonable for men to adopt if they were not biased by special interests arising from their actual positions in society. He could equally well have framed the question by asking what principles an impartial person would adopt. Where

1. R. M. Hare. 'Rules of War and Moral Philosophy', *Philosophy and Public Affairs*, Vol. 1, No. 2 (Winter, 1972), 166–81, p. 171.
2. London: Routledge & Kegan Paul, 1966.

Rawls is distinctive (except insofar as Hare takes a similar line) is in the motivational postulates that he employs. As we have seen, he rules out altruism in the original position, or (to put it more helpfully) he rules out the possession of substantive moral principles.

There is one complicating factor that must be introduced here. In 'Justice as Fairness' it appeared in a fairly straight-forward form: although the people in the original position would not have any substantive moral principles they would know that they had, so to speak, a latent sense of justice. They would know that they had the capacity to adhere to principles of justice once these had been settled upon. But in *A Theory of Justice* this 'sense of justice' has become conditional. The actors in the 'original position' no longer know that they have the capacity to stick to *whatever* principles are chosen, though they do know enough 'general psychology' to be aware that if they were to choose the 'two principles' they would be able to stick to *them*.

In *A Theory of Justice*, the question of the 'stability' of a just society occupies a large place: to the extent that Part Three could be said to have a theme this is it. A society is 'stable', in the relevant sense here, if there are adequate motives in human nature (supported by appropriate methods of child-hood socialization) to enable people to live up to the publicly recognized standards of justice without requiring a great deal of coercion. Rawls argues, for example, that the utilitarian principle is not compatible with stability because maximizing average utility may conceivably require that some be made wretched in order to make others very happy indeed. (See pages 175–8.)

The criterion of potential stability therefore sets limits on the range of principles that can be chosen by the parties in the original position. 'They cannot enter into agreements that may have consequences they cannot accept. They will avoid those that they can adhere to only with great difficulty.' (Page 176.) Unfortunately, this argument is so powerful that it seems to be in imminent danger of short-circuiting the whole elaborate argument in favour of the 'two principles'. For if (as Rawls sometimes appears to imply) they are the only principles capable of satisfying the demands of stability, that would seem to end the matter then and there. In order to avoid this premature closure of the discussion I shall, therefore, assume that the requirements of stability are compatible with a fairly wide range of possible principles.

Let us return from this excursus to the main point to be considered here: Rawls's denial of substantive moral sentiments to the actors in the original position. This has always been an essential part of the theory of 'justice as fairness' as Rawls has presented it, yet I do not think he has ever presented wholly convincing reasons for accepting the postulate. The argument, from the article 'Justice as Fairness' onwards, has been the same. Questions of justice arise only where there is conflict of interest. If there were perfect coincidence of interest there would be no disputes requiring adjudication and therefore no call to have principles of justice. This all appears to me manifestly true, but the trouble is that it does not prove that the parties in the original position should be conceived of as (in the sense defined) devoid of altruism. According to Rawls, 'when it is supposed that the parties are severally disinterested, and are not willing to have their interests sacrificed to the others, the intention is to express men's conduct and motives in cases where questions of justice arise.' (Page 129.) But what is to stop us accepting that the 'circumstances of justice' are what Rawls says they are, and then putting into the original position human beings with their actual moral notions? (This is in effect what Runciman does.) The basic logic would still be the same. In real life people disagree on moral principles because they have conflicting interests; if we put them into a situation where these conflicting interests cannot influence them, they can reach agreement.

The reason why Rawls adopts the motivational postulates he does is actually very simple, that without them there can be no 'moral geometry'. Once we allow the actors in the original position to have substantive moral notions, we have to say that in the absence of self-interested biases people would agree on this or that principle, which is not deduction but assertion. The snag, however, is that it does not tell us why we should believe that the principles adopted by 'non-altruistic' people in the original position are principles of justice. It seems likely that Rawls is worried about this himself, for it may be recalled that the book's final paragraph, of which I quoted the opening sentences, is a last attempt to deal with this question : 'why should we take any interest in [the original position], moral or otherwise?' But his answer, which stresses the value of the original position as an 'Archimedean point', mentions only those features of it that ensure that the parties cannot be influenced by their special interests arising from their own peculiar circumstances. And, although laborious textual criticism would be needed to set out the case in detail, I shall simply assert here that it appears to me that whenever Rawls tries to convince us of the virtues of the original position it is the limitations placed on knowledge on which he lays stress and not the motivational postulates.

All this, of course, has quite serious implications for the possible success of Rawls's design in *A Theory of Justice*. The cornerstone of the theory is that the principles that would be chosen in the original position, which Rawls describes as the 'most favored, or standard, interpretation' of the 'initial situation' (page 121), are necessarily principles of justice. I have now suggested that Rawls does not provide us with any good reasons for believing this to be so. Indeed, I think it is possible to put the point more strongly and say that something's being chosen in the original position would definitely not of itself guarantee that the thing chosen would be just. Thus, suppose that two people are put into an 'original position' and told that one of them is white and the other black and that in ability and training they are identical. They are also told that they have a choice of being in one of two societies. In the first (e.g. Lesotho) both will be paid £4 a week for doing the same work (for which they are trained), while in the second (e.g. the Union of South Africa) they will be paid different amounts, the white £40 a week and the black £5 a week, for doing the same work side by side. On Rawls's premises about motivation in the original position, which include the postulate that neither will be upset by relativities as such (in other words that each person's utility depends on his own income alone), both parties will clearly be rational to choose to be in the second society rather than the first. But the arrangements of the second society are not just because paying people different amounts for doing the same work side by side on account of their having different coloured skins or more generally being of different 'races' is inherently unjust.[3]

Has Rawls a reply to this? Since he does not deal with the matter in these terms, we have to put the question by asking whether a reply can be constructed. I think Rawls could salvage the theory, at this point at least, along the following lines. He might accept that the example does show a case in which an unjust outcome would be chosen in a situation having the features of the 'original position'. He could also accept the general conclusion arising from this, that choice under circumstances incorporating the specified constraints on information and motivation does not guarantee justice. But he could rally his forces after this retreat by saying that for his own purposes he does not need to maintain any proposition as broad as that anyway. All he has to be committed to is that *when the choice to be made is of the principles for judging the basic institutions and laws of a society* the choices made in the original position will coincide with the requirements of justice.

The parties in the original position have available to them, as we shall see in subsequent chapters, a body of 'psychological generalizations' and some elements of social and economic theory. This information enables them to predict (in certain respects) the implications of choosing one principle rather than another. Thus, for example, they will know about the need for providing incentives to get people into the right jobs and get them to work hard at them, and they will be willing to permit inequalities of this kind. But they will also know that racial discrimination of the kind in the example can never in real life be optimal for a society and will therefore rule it out.

Such a line of argument, which we can find at many places in the book, obviously places a great weight on the facts of human psychology and the constraints of social 'laws' to produce the right answer. And of course it still does not explain *why* there should be such a coincidence between the choices that would be made in the 'original position' and our intuitive notions of justice as to enable the two to be brought into 'reflective equilibrium'. But it leaves us with a programme of work. We can ask whether Rawls's 'two principles' *would* be

3. This example is a more circumstantial and elaborate version of one given by Mr. J. L. Mackie in a paper delivered in Oxford in November 1972.

chosen in the original position and we can also, and independently, ask whether we think they are a good idea. If the answer to both questions were 'yes', we should even then not know why this was so, but it would surely be a philosophically interesting and important thing to have established. And even in the absence of any *a priori* reason to expect a coincidence, we might be willing to go in for a Rawlsian process of *tâtonnement* towards 'reflective equilibrium' if we found that the principles that would be chosen in the original position coincided at essential points but not all points with our intuitive notions of justice.

3

PRIMARY GOODS AND THE
THIN THEORY OF THE GOOD

THE two principles of justice, with their ramifying clauses and the various interrelations within them and between them, may have appeared formidable enough, but I assure the reader that they are simplicity itself compared with what lies behind them. If we want to know how being 'worst off' is defined (worst off in terms of what?) and if we want to know why the rights covered by the first principle should have priority, we must study Rawls's theory of 'primary goods', and to do that we have to take account of the 'thin theory of the good'. Until this is done we cannot even say exactly what the principles of justice mean, let alone ask whether we like them or whether they are really deducible from the original position. The present chapter is therefore devoted to this essential investigation.

The two principles of justice have different subject-matters. The first is concerned with civil and political rights, the second with material or non-material interests. But the two are unified at a deeper level within the theory. The rights and the interests all either *are* or *are means to* members of the set of primary goods. The alternation in this statement makes life difficult but is, as I understand it, an accurate statement of the position. It would obviously be easier if we could either identify the rights and interests with primary goods or if we could say that all the rights and interests are means to primary goods which can be independently defined. As it is there are both kinds of relationship, and anyone reading *A Theory of Justice* is bound at this point to start asking questions like: do any of the rights connect to any of the same primary goods as the interests, and if so do they connect in the same way or differently? He may at this point notice wisps of steam beginning to come from his ears, and this will increase when he adds the question how all this connects up with the 'thin theory of the good'.

Before things get completely out of hand, I think it will be prudent to stand back a bit and ask in a general kind of way what Rawls is up to in this part of his theory, which, because of its great complexity, occupies a substantial proportion of the book. To answer this question we must go back to the discussion in the last chapter of the original position. It will be recalled that the parties in the original position do not know what their 'conception of the good' is, and this includes their tastes in food or company, their religious and other beliefs and in brief all those factors which make one person want some things out of life and another person different things. All they know in this area are some general facts about human psychology.

Now suppose that you take some people and put them behind the 'veil of ignorance' so that they don't know what they like doing, what is important to them, and, in a word, what they want. You then tell them to come up with some principles to regulate their life together. It seems difficult to avoid the conclusion that whatever principles they agree on will have to be defined in terms of satisfying wants, for wants (content unknown) are apparently left as the only common factor. This does not say anything about *what* principles they will accept, it simply specifies what these principles will be about. We are leaving open the question whether they will go for the maximization of the total sum of want-satisfaction, regardless of how it is distributed, or for the equalization of want-satisfaction, or for maximizing the amount of want-satisfaction of the person with the least, or for any of a hundred others, or any kind of pluralistic cocktail of any combination of them.

In terms of a distinction which I drew in *Political Argument*[1] and which Rawls takes over, we are saying that the actors in the original position will come up with principles that are 'want-regarding' rather than 'ideal-regarding'. Since the point sometimes causes difficulties, I trust it will be apparent from the way that we have arrived at this point that the 'wants'

1. London: Routledge & Kegan Paul, 1965.

included here may be of any kind including the most exalted personal or spiritual ideals. The want-regarding/ideal-regarding distinction is not based on what it is that people want; it is based on how what they want is treated for the purpose of social evaluation. That is to say, if you assimilate all wants of whatever kind and evaluate states of affairs in terms of the overall amount and/or distribution of want-satisfaction you are adhering to a want-regarding position. If you do anything else, in other words if you discriminate among wants of different kinds for purposes of evaluation then you are an adherent of the ideal-regarding view. The basis of discrimination among wants can be of absolutely any kind. Obvious candidates, which have or have in the past had actual adherents are the origins of the want (how the person came to have it), whether it is selfish or not, whether it is (in the judgement of the evaluator) an enlightened want or not, whether or not the want is compatible with the teachings of a religion believed in by the evaluator, or (more generally) whether the want is an 'intrinsically good' one to be fulfilled or not.

To the best of my knowledge, the case against treating wants as the units of social evaluation has never been set forth systematically, although it seems to be true both that want-regarding notions underlie many theoretical and practical discussions of politics, economics, etc., and at the same time that the implications of a want-regarding view are repugnant to many people. It would take me too far out of my way to discuss the matter in detail, but I shall mention three possible sticking points. First, it may be felt that there is something fundamentally wrong in treating alike for the purposes of calculation such diverse things as wants for personal gratification of oneself, the desire to give others pleasure, ambitions to contribute to the world's stock of truth and beauty, aspirations towards spiritual improvement and enlightenment, and so on. Second, carrying this a stage further, it may be considered inconceivable that any set of principles which does not discriminate among wants (except of course in terms of relative intensity) could give rise to implications which could be conscientiously endorsed. And finally, one might actually carry out the exercise of constructing the most hopeful-looking set of want-regarding principles one can think of and discover that when this set of principles is applied to actual or hypothetical situations the implications are indeed morally unacceptable.

Now I said before beginning the present topic that my object was to stand back from the intricacies of Rawls's theory of 'primary goods' and the 'thin theory of the good' that underlies it, in order to ask what the point of the whole business was. I am now in a position to give the answer. This apparatus is designed to get Rawls out of an awkward dilemma. On the one hand, he does not like the implications of the want-regarding view, and wishes, for example, to be able to say that the desire of someone to practice his religion freely should have priority over the desire of another man to stop him, even if the second man's desire is more intense than the first's, or if those who want to worship are outnumbered by those who want to suppress and each person has the same intensity of desire for what he wants. Yet at the same time he wishes to derive principles of justice from an original position which, by denying the actors specific information about themselves, seems to lead inexorably towards the formulation of principles in want-regarding terms. In my view the connection *is* inexorable. The lengthiness and complexity of Rawl's manoeuvres are, I believe, an illustration of the slogan 'The impossible takes a little longer'. If you put nothing but wants in at the beginning you cannot get anything but wants out at the end. Conversely, if you do succeed in validly getting something else out at the end this can only be because you put something else in at the beginning.

What Rawls in fact produces is a want-regarding conception at one remove. But the only thing that keeps it at one remove is *a priori* psychology. The crux is that if the psychological premises are correct then a straight want-regarding theory will produce morally acceptable results anyway; it is only to the extent that the *a priori* psychology is actually false that there can be any divergence between the practical implications of Rawls's two-stage theory and a correctly applied want-regarding theory otherwise corresponding to it. The general form of reasoning that we find at this point runs like this: (1) want-regarding principles would sometimes have unacceptable practical implications; (2) these implications can be avoided if we make sufficiently strenuous psychological generalizations; (3) therefore let us postulate that the parties in the 'original position' have access to psychological generalizations which embody these assumptions.

Rawls, when discussing the want-regarding/ideal-regarding issue, says that his theory is not a want-regarding one. Except in a secondary way I do not think this is true. He describes the attributes of a want-regarding theory accurately enough in general terms but it appears to me that the main ground he adduces for saying his theory is not a want-regarding one rests on a mistake about the implications of a want-regarding theory. Since the point is of some importance I shall quote him almost in full.

We may define ideal-regarding principles as those which are not want-regarding principles. That is, they do not take as the only relevant features the overall amount of want-satisfaction and the way in which it is distributed among persons. Now in terms of this distinction, the principles of justice . . . are ideal-regarding principles. They do not abstract from the aims of desires and hold that satisfactions are of equal value when they are equally intense and pleasurable (the meaning of Bentham's remark that . . . pushpin is as good as poetry). As we have seen (§41), a certain ideal is embedded in the principles of justice, and the fulfillment of desires incompatible with these principles has no value at all. Moreover we are to encourage certain traits of character, especially a sense of justice. (Pages 326–7.)

The last point I accept. But it should be noted that from Rawls's official standpoint character traits cannot be encouraged as desirable in themselves, because this would involve a 'full theory of the good', and the introduction of such a theory constitutes 'perfectionism'. The only justification that can be given for encouraging a sense of justice is that this will tend to increase the incidence of conformity with the 'two principles of justice' which are themselves (if I am right) at one remove want-regarding. We may indeed still wish to say that *any* advocacy of encouraging certain character traits at the expense of others makes a theory ideal-regarding, and strictly speaking I think this would be accurate. But we should then be aware that we are adopting a criterion of an ideal-regarding theory which has the consequence that no evaluative theory that has ever been put forward can be described as want-regarding, and this has the unfortunate consequence for Rawls of destroying the distinction that he wishes to draw between his own theory and Benthamite utilitarianism. For even the most hardboiled utilitarian has something to say about encouraging certain traits of character. Indeed, oddly enough, Rawls himself, in another context, makes great play with the fact that the 'classical utilitarians' always stressed heavily the importance of inculcating sentiments of benevolence: 'Their conception of justice is threatened with instability unless sympathy and benevolence can be widely and intensely cultivated.' (Page 178.) This is obviously a precise parallel with Rawls's statement that on his theory a sense of justice would be encouraged, for benevolence is to utilitarianism as a sense of justice is to Rawls's theory. Utilitarianism, as he observes, is universal benevolence and therefore needs benevolent people to make it work with a minimum of coercion. In a precisely parallel way, he says that the reason for inculcating a sense of justice is that this will if successful enable a Rawlsian society to operate with a minimum of coercion. We can thus say that, yes, Rawls's theory is ideal-regarding—fully as much as Bentham's!

This, however, is a side-issue. The main point is the nature of the 'two principles of justice' themselves. Do these constitute a want-regarding theory, in the sense in which Bentham's principle of utility undeniably does, or not? In his argument here it seems to me that Rawls is guilty of the fallacy of affirming the consequent. Ideal-regarding theories, by definition, hold that the fulfilment of some wants is of less value than the fulfilment of other wants, or even of no value at all. This, as we have seen, may be in virtue of their origins, their content or anything else about them. But it is a fallacy to say that any theory which holds that the fulfilment of some wants is (in a very special sense) without value is an ideal-regarding theory. It is not an ideal-regarding theory if all it says is that the fulfilment of desires *incompatible with the criteria of distribution laid down in the theory* is without value. Indeed, that is precisely what is meant when one says that a want-regarding theory is not purely aggregative but includes distributive criteria.

In other words, we can say that every want-regarding theory which does not either consist of, or at least include as one principle of evaluation, simple aggregative utilitarianism has exactly the property that Rawls claims for his own theory.[2] It may be pointed out, indeed, that some criteria go further than Rawls's criterion of maximizing the position of the worst-off in denying the value of want-satisfaction inconsistent with their requirements. On Rawls's criterion it is simply of no value, but on, for example, the criterion of equality, an increase in some people's want-satisfaction can actually be of negative value, that is to say it makes the situation evaluatively worse than it was before. For if someone above the average goes further above the average this produces a decrease in the degree of equality. Yet this does not make an egalitarian criterion inherently ideal-regarding.

I should make it clear that I am not (though I may appear to be) placing a heavy weight of interpretation on the passage from Rawls that I quoted, though the meaning I have attributed to him is, I believe, consistent with everything in that passage. But it will be noted that he says in the passage 'As we have seen (§41) . . .', and it is the content of that section which gives me confidence that I have correctly interpreted what he has in mind. For, if we turn to § 41, the only relevant passage we find is the following: 'desires for things that are inherently unjust, or that cannot be satisfied except by the violation of just arrangements, have no weight. There is no value in fulfilling these wants and the social system should discourage them.' (Page 261.) The last clause here contains the secondary point that I discussed first. The rest of the quotation makes the observation that I have been taking to lie at the core of Rawls's argument for the ideal-regarding character of his theory.

At the end of the paragraph which I have been discussing in the last few pages, Rawls throws in an entirely new argument for the ideal-regarding character of the theory. (This cumulation of brief arguments, presented without any attempt to relate them, is highly typical of Rawls's way of proceeding.)

2. For the sake of complete accuracy it should be added that if there are several principles including the utilitarian one in a lexicographic ordering (what I have been calling informally a 'relation of absolute priority') the utilitarian one must come first, and if the relation is defined by an indifference-surface (what I have been calling, following Rawls, 'pluralism') then the shape of the surface must be such that movement outward along the utilitarian axis must always result in a movement upward on the surface, all else remaining the same.

The new argument is contained in two sentences. 'In fact, the principles of justice do not even mention the amount or the distribution of welfare but refer only to the distribution of liberties and the other primary goods. At the same time they manage to define an ideal of the person without invoking a prior standard of human excellence.' (Page 327.) But this is entirely consistent with my claim that Rawls's theory is a want-regarding theory at one remove. Perhaps it is worth repeating here the point that Rawls is in a Catch-22 situation: if the system is consistent and its premises are want-regarding the principles must in the last analysis be want-regarding; but if Rawls is correct in stating that the principles are ideal-regarding there is either an inconsistency in the system or the premises do 'invoke a prior standard of human excellence'.

I have now, I hope, explained sufficiently what is the purpose of the theory of primary goods, and also why the enterprise appears to me to be doomed to failure from the outset. I must now, in the remainder of this chapter, follow through Rawls's theory of primary goods and also the 'thin theory of the good' on which it rests. The logical order of exposition is to lay out the 'thin theory of the good' first, and that is the order I shall follow. One of the most difficult features of *A Theory of Justice* is that Rawls reverses this order. The discussion of primary goods comes where it is needed for the construction of the two principles of justice but the 'thin theory of the good' is delayed until Part Three. The relationship of dependence is as follows. The primary goods are defined as things which any rational person would desire to have, and therefore it can be deduced that the actors in the original position will wish to secure them for themselves. But the actors in the original position do not know what it is in particular that they want, so how can they know what things are a means to fulfilling their desires? The object of the 'thin theory of good' is to enable Rawls to say that, although different men may want different things, there are certain standard features of wants and these provide the basis for arguing to standardized means to want-fulfilment.

The 'thin theory of the good' is subtle and ramified; its exposition takes up a tenth of the whole of *A Theory of Justice*, that is, well over a third of the length of the present work. It contains many thought-provoking details and will no doubt be much discussed by philosophers. I can here only highlight the points that are essential to the development of the theory of primary goods. Fortunately, the central notion is quite simple. Rawls attributes to each man what he calls a 'rational plan', which defines his principal goals in life. A man's 'good' is then said by Rawls to consist in 'the successful execution of a rational plan of life' (page 433). The 'thin theory of the good' is concerned with what can be deduced from this proposition and other subsidiary propositions (to be mentioned below) which similarly abstract from the content of people's wants.

Now if we drop the word 'rational' and leave only 'plan', and if (as Rawls urges—see pages 423–4) we discount the 'planning and calculating' overtones of the word 'plan', we are left essentially with the proposition that a man's good is to be conceived as lying in his getting more rather than less of whatever things it is that he happens to want. Everything therefore turns on what can be extracted from the concept of 'rationality'. But here Catch-22 pops up again, for what can be extracted can only be what is put in. Struggle as he may—and Rawls struggles valiantly—he cannot free himself from the fundamental incompatibility between the kind of premises which he chooses to adopt and the kind of conclusions he wishes to reach. The premises, the conclusions, the demands of consistency: one must be sacrificed. For a long time it looks as if consistency will be abandoned but at the last Rawls draws back and drops his conclusions. But this does not prevent him from using them as the foundation of the theory of 'primary goods'.

We can watch this process at work clearly if we follow through Rawls's most important attempt to set substantive limitations on the possible patterns of human desire: the so-called 'Aristotelian principle'. This principle states that 'other things being equal, human beings enjoy the exercise of their realized capacities (their innate or trained abilities), and this enjoyment increases the more the capacity is realized, or the greater its complexity.' (Page 426.) This statement is glossed immediately as follows: 'The intuitive idea here is that human beings take more pleasure in doing something as they become more proficient at it, and of two activities they do equally well, they prefer the one calling on a larger repertoire of more intricate and subtle discriminations. ... Thus the principle says that someone who can do both generally prefers playing chess to playing checkers, and that he would rather study algebra than arithmetic.' (Page 426.)

The problem posed by the 'Aristotelian principle' is pretty evident. Either it is an empirical generalization or it is a partially constitutive definition of 'rationality'. If it is an empirical generalization it appears to me open to serious doubt. Moreover, Rawls requires not merely that it should be true but that it should be so unquestionably true that the actors in the original position will treat it as an axiom in their reasoning about the choice of principles. Alternatively, let us suppose that it is put forward as a partially constitutive definition of 'rationality'. This would mean that a man whose choice ran counter to it would be said not to have a 'rational plan'. For example, somebody with a moderately well-developed palate for wine who preferred most of the time to drink beer would have to be called irrational, since less discrimination is involved in drinking beer than drinking wine. We must, then, say that, contrary to Rawls's professed intentions, a substantive idea of human excellence is being advanced under cover of the neutral-appearing concept of rationality.

Rawls in the end comes down on the side of empirical generalization. He asks us to imagine an intelligent man 'whose only pleasure is to count blades of grass in various geometrically shaped areas such as park squares and well-trimmed lawns. ... The definition of the good forces us to admit that the good for this man is indeed counting blades of grass, or more accurately, his good is determined by a plan that gives an especially prominent place to this activity.' He goes on to comment: 'I mention this fanciful case only to show that the correctness of the definition of a person's good in terms of the rational plan for him does not require the truth of the Aristotelian principle. The definition is satisfactory, I believe, even if the principle should prove inaccurate, or fail altogether.' (Pages 432–3.) But without the 'Aristotelian principle' the concept of rationality does not have much of a cutting edge. Although Rawls devotes a section to the discussion of what he calls 'deliberative rationality' (§64) all this comes down to really is that the plan should be chosen with care: it does not set limits to what can be the content of a 'rational plan' in the way that the 'Aristotelian principle', if it were accepted, would do.

If the 'Aristotelian principle' is an empirical generalization, it must be true, and unquestionably true, to operate as a premise in the original position. Although Rawls appeared to concede in the passage I have just quoted that the principle might be wrong, he in fact relies on its being true and being available as a 'psychological generalization' in the original position. His justification, which follows on from the quotation given and ends the section, runs as follows: 'But by assuming the principle we seem able to account for what things are recognized as good for human beings taking them as they are. Moreover, since this principle ties in with the primary good of self-respect, it turns out to have a central position in the moral psychology underlying justice as fairness.' (Page 433.)

The 'moreover' here is breathtaking. It means that an additional argument in favour of the 'Aristotelian principle' is that it is an essential foundation of Rawls's theory of justice. If anything this fact should surely tell in the other direction. Disregarding this, we are left with an empirical assertion which may be broadly true or may not, but surely is not so clearly, incontrovertibly and universally true as to form an axiom for reasoning in the 'original position'. One of Rawls's criteria of rationality is that in taking important decisions one should play safe so as to minimize subsequent regret if things turn out badly. I would certainly sympathize with someone in the original position who took the line that it would be unreasonable to base his choice of principles on the assumption that if he were capable of chess and algebra he would prefer them to less cerebral pursuits.

It seems to me that Rawls allows himself far too easy a victory by choosing as his one hypothetical counter-example the ludicrous one that he does, implying that such bizarre possibilities constitute the only exceptions—though some hobbies are not much less limited in scope, if it comes to that. My own inclination is to think that the 'Aristotelian principle' is, as a matter of fact, false for most people most of the time. It is probably least untrue for the middle-class Americans described by David

Riesman in *The Lonely Crowd* who have turned the puritan ethic into one of a duty to fill their 'leisure' time with strenuous and 'fulfilling' activities, and who search their consciences to see if they are enjoying themselves enough.

It is to be emphasized that the question posed by the 'Aristotelian principle' is not whether people get some satisfaction out of doing difficult things, but whether everyone's central aims in life are bound up with the exercise of the most complex faculties, as against (say) eating, drinking, making love or watching television. Recall that this is not a question of what people ought to want, what would make them happy, what would express the best kind of character, etc. As Rawls recognizes, such questions involve the introduction of specific conceptions of exellence—a 'full theory' rather than a 'thin theory' of the good. Like John Stuart Mill (whose idea of the 'higher pleasures' is closely similar) Rawls is committed to the attempt to get a differentiation among aims from want-regarding premises, and in both cases, it appears to me, the attempt founders on the' facts.

Without the 'Aristotelian principle', the 'thin theory of the good' amounts to little more, as I have pointed out, than the definition of a man's good as getting as much as possible of what he wants. The general conception of primary goods requires no more than this; but when we come on to specifying which things are primary goods and especially to ranking primary goods in importance we shall see that the 'Aristotelian principle' is needed. The idea, then, underlying the notion of primary goods is that there are certain things which are means to a very wide range of ends and which as a result it is rational for anybody to want, whatever his particular ambitions, tastes or beliefs might be.

The most obvious examples are wealth and power, often called 'interests'. If we define power as the capacity to get other people to do what you want and wealth as the ability to obtain goods and services that you want, it is evident that they are means to the satisfaction of an extremely wide range of wants. There are few wants the extent or probability of whose satisfaction cannot be to any degree increased by the possession of power or wealth. Even if your aim is spiritual advancement, money can buy you the leisure to practise it and any aids you need from a set of beads to a trip to India. What is perhaps more important is a further point, though it is not a point that Rawls makes, and would not fit in with his theory. With much more confidence than we could ever have in the 'Aristotelian principle' we can assert the 'psychological generalization' that there are certain ends which really are central to the lives of all human beings: food, shelter, security against physical danger and (the Hobbesian addendum) above all some security of continuing to enjoy them in the future. Wealth and power are means to these ends and it is this as much as the range of wants to which they are means that gives them such significance.

What is distinctive about Rawls is not that he includes wealth and power among the primary goods—he would be unique if he did not—but that he plays them down, first by adding other primary goods and second by saying that these other primary goods are (subject to a minimum level of wealth being reached) of infinitely greater importance. The other primary goods, then, are the traditional liberal civil rights (freedom of thought and conscience and the rule of law) plus the right to participate in political decision-making. There is a further primary good, which plays a vital role in Rawls's theory, and that is the primary good of 'self-respect'. I shall explain what the meaning of this is in a moment but first I think it is worth emphasizing that, in calling civil and political rights 'primary goods', Rawls is not simply saying that the parties in the original position would wish to guarantee these rights, for they might do this if they saw them only as essential means to the preservation of a just distribution of wealth and power. This is indeed how the importance of political rights is often argued for. What Rawls is here committing himself to is the view that civil and political rights are themselves the direct and immediate means to the realization of central goals in life held by (almost) all people. We can see here, and even more clearly in the priority asserted for the primary goods other than 'interests', the part played by the 'Aristotelian principle'.

The primary good of self-respect is defined as a person's sense that his plan of life is a worthy one and its fulfilment is of value. Exactly what this in turn means is not too clear. In particular it is never made quite explicit whether Rawls includes conceptually in 'self-respect' that the worth of a person's plan should be avowed by others or whether it is regarded by him as a universally true empirical proposition that self-respect requires social validation. I shall discuss the point in Chapter 5 when I ask where social status fits into Rawls's theory. For now the point to notice is that the primary good of self-respect has a different relation to the first principle of justice from that which the civil and political rights have. They are themselves the stuff whose distribution the first principle deals with. But there is no mention of self-respect in the definition of the principles of justice. Rather, self-respect is a primary good to which the first principle, and to some extent the part of the second principle demanding equal opportunity, are means. According to Rawls, the relationship is delightfully straight-forward. The equal distribution of self-respect is said to be provided for so long as civil and political liberties are equally available to all and so long as no one is debarred from compet-ing for offices and positions carrying advantages of wealth or power. I shall, at a number of points later in this study, have occasion to remark upon the archaic quality of Rawls's liberal-ism. This is an excellent example of what I have in mind. For Rawls, the obstacles to the achievement of equality of self-respect lie entirely in legally-prescribed inequalities of civil and political rights. (The right to compete for lucrative or power-ful positions may be for most purposes assimilated to other civil rights, within Rawls's theory.) That equality of self-respect may be as much or more hindered by inequalities of wealth or power themselves apparently does not occur to him. Certainly he does not regard the first part of the second principle as being underwritten by the primary good of self-respect in the way that the first principle and the second part of the second principle are. If it were, he would be embarrassed in putting it at the end of the queue.

The business of this chapter is now completed. In the next two chapters I shall set out the two principles of justice, and after that I shall discuss their derivation from the original position. Before doing this, however, I should like to quote Rawls's own explanation of the way in which the various parts of his theory fit together, since I fear that in the complexities of the 'thin theory of the good', the theory of primary goods, and the relation of both to the principles and their derivation, the thread may have got lost.

The index of well-being and the expectations of representative men [in specifying the content of the two principles of justice] are specified in terms of primary goods. Rational individuals, whatever else they want, desire certain things as prerequisites for carrying out their plans of life. Other things equal, they prefer a wider to a narrower liberty and opportunity, and a greater rather than a smaller share [this should read 'amount'—B. B.] of wealth and income [and power—B. B.]. That these things are good seems clear enough. But I have also said that self-respect and a sure confidence in the sense of one's own worth is perhaps the most important primary good. And this suggestion has been used in the argument for the two principles of justice (§29). [The claim made in this section is that the two principles of justice embody the Kantian idea of treating everyone as an end in himself rather than as a means to the satisfaction of other people's desires.—B. B.] Thus the initial definition of expectations solely by reference to such things as liberty and wealth is provisional; it is necessary to include other kinds of primary goods and these raise deeper questions. Obviously an account of the good is required for this; and it must be the thin theory. . . .

Summing up these points, we need what I have called the thin theory of the good to explain the rational preference for primary goods and to explicate the notion of rationality underlying the choice of principles in the original position. This theory is necessary to support the requisite premises from which the principles of justice are derived. (Pages 396–7; ellipses cover one omitted paragraph.)

4

THE FIRST PRINCIPLE OF JUSTICE

First Principle. Each person is to have an equal right to the most extensive total system of equal basic liberties compatible with a similar system of liberty for all. (Page 302.)

There are three points that call for comment here. First, what is the significance of talking about a '*total system* of equal basic liberties'? Why not simply say, as in 'Justice as Fairness', 'equal liberty'? The answer is that Rawls thinks of the various liberties as capable of occurring (within limits) independently of one another, and suggests that, if maximizing one is inconsistent with maximizing the others, different proportions of the various liberties should be combined in such a way as to make the 'total system' one of as much liberty, equally distributed, as possible. Rawls gives little usable guidance about the way to aggregate the different liberties so as to arrive at an estimate of the total amount of liberty generated by alternative combinations of these different liberties; and I shall not pursue the question in this book, although it would obviously be of crucial importance if one were seriously to attempt to apply the 'two principles of justice' in a real society. Rawls tells us simply that since the liberties may conflict 'the delegates to a constitutional convention, or the members of the legislature, must decide how the various liberties are to be specified so as to yield the best total system of equal liberty. They have to balance one liberty against another.' (Page 203.) The only other information he gives is that 'this scheme [of liberty] is always to be assessed from the standpoint of the representative equal citizen.' (Page 204.)

The second question we have to ask is what is covered by

the 'total system of equal basic liberties'? What exactly is the specification of 'basic liberties'? Rawls sets them out under three headings.

One basic liberty is what Rawls describes as 'political liberty': 'the principle of equal liberty, when applied to the political procedure defined by the constitution, I shall refer to as the principle of (equal) participation. It requires that all citizens are to have an equal right to take part in, and to determine the outcome of, the constitutional process that establishes the laws with which they are to comply.' (Page 221.) I shall discuss §36, on 'Political Justice and the Constitution', and §37, on 'Limitations on Participation', in detail in Chapters 13 and 14; so, having quoted Rawls's description of this basic liberty, I shall postpone any further consideration of it.

Another basic liberty is dealt with by Rawls in the following §38, 'The Rule of Law'. The description of the content of the 'rule of law' has no surprises: it includes (1) the principle that 'ought implies can', and therefore that laws should require only possible behaviour (see pages 236–7), (2) 'the precept that similar cases be treated similarly' (pages 237–8), (3) 'the precept that there is no offence without a law', which 'demands that laws be known and expressly promulgated' etc. (pages 237–8), and finally (4) 'precepts defining the notion of natural justice' which require for example that 'judges must be fair and impartial, and no man may judge his own case' (pages 238–9). The point to get clear is that the 'rule of law' as set out here does not in any important respect restrict the possible content of law. As Rawls says, it is 'justice as regularity' (page 235). Thus, it would be perfectly consistent with the 'rule of law' to have a precisely drafted statute forbidding the public worship of any religion (or any religion except one), one making homosexual behaviour among consenting adults a criminal offence, and so on almost indefinitely. All the traditional 'liberal' personal rights therefore have to come in the remaining category, but it is not at all clear that they do.

The basic ideas here are set out in §33, 'Equal Liberty of Conscience', and certain points are then taken up in the two subsequent sections. The difficulty presented by these sections to the reader can be explained as follows. As the title of the section suggests, the principle involved is defined in terms of liberty of conscience, that is to say, the liberty to do what you believe to be right, subject to the requirements of 'the state's interest in public order and security' (page 212). And all the arguments put forward are related to liberty of conscience understood in this way. But much of the content of personal freedom as advocated by liberals consists of having the right to do things which one wants to do, without believing that it is a matter of religious duty or conscientious conviction. Does Rawls somehow cover these by his discussion of 'equal liberty of conscience'?

There is one passage, over two hundred pages after that discussion, in which he appears to assume that he has indeed established the right to do what one wants (and not only what one believes one *ought* to do) subject to one's actions not causing 'injury' to others. The context is, yet again, that of attacking utilitarianism because of what are maintained to be the possible implications of utilitarian calculation. 'For example, assume that the larger part of society has an abhorrence for certain religious or sexual practices, and regards them as an abomination. This feeling is so intense that it is not enough that these practices be kept from the public view; the very thought that these things are going on is enough to arouse the majority to anger and hatred.' (Page 450.) Utilitarianism may therefore, Rawls says, 'justify harsh repressive measures against actions that cause no social injury' (page 450). But, according to Rawls, this could not happen under the two principles of justice because 'the satisfaction of these feelings has no value that can be put in the scales against the claims of equal liberty. To have a complaint against the conduct and belief of others we must show that their actions injure us, or that the institutions that authorize what they do treat us unjustly. And this means that we must appeal to the principles that we would acknowledge in the original position. Against these principles neither the intensity of feeling nor its being shared by the majority counts for anything.' (Page 450.)

This seems clear enough, at any rate so long as we think we know the criteria for 'injury'. Rawls nowhere enlarges on the passage I have quoted, and there is nothing similar in the earlier sections, where the only constraints mentioned are those of 'public order and security' already mentioned. We must therefore interpret 'injury' for ourselves and I think it is fairly plain from the context that 'injury' should be understood to refer to the kind of physical hurt, monetary loss or substantial nuisance (noise, smell, reduction of light, etc.) which give grounds for a civil action in legal systems such as those of Britain and the U.S.A. The criterion for intervention proposed is, in other words, of the general kind put forward (though not completely consistently followed) by the Wolfenden Report[1] such that the only problems for the law to deal with in relation to homosexuality and prostitution are public indecency and soliciting respectively.

The extension of the sphere of personal liberty from matters of conscience is made explicit by the yoking together of 'religious or sexual practices'—provided of course we assume that deviant sexual practices are not for most people who perform them thought to be enjoined by religious or conscientious convictions. Indeed, this phrase 'religious or sexual practices' lends a particular aptness to Lucas's comment on the Wolfenden Report: 'The absolute privilege which the early Protestants claimed for a man's spiritual relation with God, the modern liberals claim for a man's sexual relationship with his fellow men and women. A man's soul was once his impregnable fortress: and now at least an Englishman's bed is his castle.'[2]

The problem is, as I mentioned, that the earlier sections do not in fact seem to lay the groundwork for such a doctrine of personal liberty by showing that it would be chosen in the original position and it is not at all evident there that Rawls even believes this to have been done. Thus, in introducing his discussion of 'equal liberty of conscience' he says: 'The reasoning in this case can be generalized to apply to other freedoms, although not always with the same force. Turning then to liberty of conscience, it seems evident that the parties must choose principles that secure the integrity of their religious and moral freedom.' (Page 206; the same point is made in almost identical words after the argument on page 209.) But no attempt is made anywhere in the book actually to do the 'generalizing'.

1. Report of the Committee on Homosexual Offences and Prostitution, 1957, Cmnd 247.
2. J. R. Lucas, *Principles of Politics* (Oxford: Clarendon Press, 1966), p. 342.

It cannot be known exactly how Rawls thinks it would go, but the reiterated admission that the arguments for liberty of conscience would not always have the 'same force' when applied to other matters is surely a significant one. In fact, I am unable to see any obvious way of generalizing Rawls's argument since it appears to me to depend essentially on a claim about the distinctive features of religious and moral convictions *as against* other interests. It therefore hardly lends itself to being generalized *to* other interests. 'An individual recognizing religious and moral obligations regards them as binding absolutely in the sense that he cannot qualify his fulfillment of them for the sake of promoting his other interests.' (Page 207.) Although in the original position the parties do not of course know what particular religious or moral views they hold, they know they are likely to hold some; and 'the general knowledge available to the parties' (page 207) includes the information that if they have moral or religious views they will hold them with this kind of absolute priority over all mere wants. Thus the 'actuarial calculations' of the utilitarian 'calculus of social interest' (page 207) are pre-empted on the strength of the psychological generalizations known by the parties in the original position. We see, then, that the reason why, under the 'two principles of justice', it could be said that 'the satisfaction of these feelings of abhorrence has no value that can be put in the scales against equal liberty', is simply that they have been decided in advance to be less important. But the argument (whether it is correct or not is beside the point at present) has been made out only in relation to matters of religion and conscience, not other actions which might produce a reaction of 'abhorrence' in the majority of the members of the society.

Is it possible to conceive how the argument in favour of the parties in the original position guaranteeing liberty of religion and conscience might be extended to the rest of the items in the liberal catalogue such as sexual liberty? As far as I can see the only way in which this could be done would be to say that the parties in the original position have access to a much more sweeping 'psychological generalization' than that attributed to them by Rawls, namely that *any* desire the fulfilment of which does not do any injury to others is liable to be felt so strongly that it would be irrational to permit the possibility that its fulfilment might be hampered if it was abhorred sufficiently strongly by enough people in the society. The trouble with this 'psychological generalization' is twofold. First, what it gains in being broadened to produce the desired conclusions it loses in decreased plausibility. And, second, it seems at the same time too narrow in that there seems no *a priori* reason to suppose that if someone does have a desire whose fulfilment is of absolutely central importance to his life it will necessarily be one whose fulfilment cannot possibly cause any 'injury' to others. And indeed we do normally accept that mild 'injury', in the form of inconvenience, can legitimately be caused to others if the gain to the person causing it is sufficiently greater. The implication of both objections is, I think, the same: that the need for a 'calculus of social interests' cannot be swept away, as Rawls supposes, by importing heroic assumptions about a universally valid hierarchy of human goals into the original position. Rational men will not be so willing to make impossible the detailed adjustment of conflicting demands. In judging between the desire of *A* to do something and the desire of *B* to have him prevented by law from doing it, they will not wish to rule out in advance the relevance of the question 'How much does *A* want to do it and how much does *B* want to stop him?' I shall return to these reflections in a more systematic way when I come to assess the general validity of Rawls's derivation of the 'two principles of justice'.

The third point that needs to be raised is what Rawls means by 'equal' in the statement of the first principle. This may appear a silly question: 'equal' means that everybody gets the same amount. And Rawls himself often contrasts the first principle, which specifies an equal distribution, with the first part of the second principle, which permits inequalities, so long as the worst-off section of the population is as well off as it can be. But in fact it appears to me that his interpretation of 'equality' is such as to commit the first principle to as much of a maximin criterion of distribution (maximizing the minimum) as the one that is explicitly stated in maximin terms.

If we take a criterion of equal distribution, and do not combine it with any other criterion, what we are committed to is that more equality is better than less equality. Thus suppose we have a cake and are commited to dividing it so that three people have an equal share. If that is all we are committed to then the condition is fulfilled if, instead of giving them a third each, we give them an eighth each and throw the remaining five-eighths away. And, since more equality is preferable to less, it is better to give them exactly an eighth each than give one a little more than a third and the other two a little less. Now Rawls does not intend to be understood in this way, which must mean that his criterion of distribution is not simply one of equality. And indeed it will be seen that in the statement of the first principle he speaks of the 'most extensive total system of equal basic liberties'. This gets in two criteria, equality and amount, but is not self-interpreting. How are these two criteria to be related to one another?

Given the stress which Rawls so often puts on the egalitarian nature of the first principle, the most natural interpretation of the phrase would perhaps be to say that of two situations, one of which is more equal than another, the more equal one is to be preferred; but if two situations are as equal as each other, the one with the higher total amount of freedom is to be preferred. Thus the amount of freedom would be of secondary importance, acting as a tie-breaker only. This might reasonably be said to define a 'greatest equal freedom' principle, and was indeed suggested in 'Justice as Fairness' when Rawls said that it would be irrational to choose a lesser rather than a greater equal freedom.

This interpretation would of course be strongly egalitarian. In the cake example it would entail that it is better for each of the three beneficiaries to get an eighth than for one to get a bit more than a third and the other two a bit less. It is not, and this is the crucial point, the interpretation that Rawls gives of the first principle. He is willing allow that there should be unequal rights so long as the liberties of those with less liberty than the rest are as extensive as it is possible for those with the least to have. Thus, as we shall see in Chapter 14, he says that it might be rational for some people to give up their equal rights to political participation in order to secure their other rights more effectively; but there is no suggestion that they would get *more* of the other rights than the rest of the population. Therefore if on the other rights they are in the same position while not possessing the political rights the others have, their total liberty must be less. (This does not depend on how the different liberties are aggregated so long as political rights have a value in the calculation.) More generally, I think he would say that a society with a mass of equally applied restrictions on personal terms ranked lower on the first principle than one slightly less equal but with a much lower overall level of restriction.

If we reflect for a moment on the original position we can, I suggest, see that it drives Rawls towards a maximin criterion in the first principle as well as the second. For in the original position, as we know, the parties are seeking to get into a position to further their 'good', which requires gaining as much as possible of the primary goods; and they are mutually disinterested, which means that the amount of primary goods that others have does not concern them. They neither envy those with more than themselves nor pity those with less. But these conditions surely entail quite strictly that the parties in the original position cannot be concerned with the distribution of primary goods considered purely as a distribution. What, according to Rawls, they are after is to ensure as much as possible for themselves.[3] This means that the first principle cannot be truly egalitarian, and in practice Rawls treats it as a maximin.

It is curious to notice that whenever Rawls defends the view that the first principle, as he interprets it, really is egalitarian, he puts forward an argument which would be as valid in relation to a maximin criterion as an egalitarian one. His argument is that the first principle is egalitarian because it denies the possibility that a decrease in one person's liberty might be justified on the grounds that it increases somebody else's more and thus increases the sum total of liberty. This is a case of affirming the consequent rather similar to that which was involved in Rawls's argument to show that the two principles of justice are ideal-regarding. An egalitarian principle has the implication that one person's amount of the stuff in question cannot be justifiably reduced simply on the grounds that the total amount of the stuff will thereby be increased. But it does

---

3. This is why, in the quotation that ended the previous chapter, I said that 'share' should read 'amount'. Rawls makes it clear that people are not to be considered as being interested in their share, that is to say how much they have *compared with others*.

not follow that any principle with this implication is an egalitarian one. The same can be said to be implied by a maximin criterion, as Rawls on other occasions points out.

5

THE SECOND PRINCIPLE
OF JUSTICE

Second Principle. Social and economic inequalities are to be
arranged so that they are both: (*a*) to the greatest benefit of the
least advantaged, consistent with the just savings principle,
and (*b*) attached to offices and positions open to all under conditions of fair equality of opportunity. (Page 302.)

I shall take the two parts of this principle in turn, and begin
by disposing of the clause about the 'just savings principle'. The
point here is that the maximization of the income of the worst-
off section of the population might entail spending nothing on
investment, and this would make the next generation worse off
than the current one. A rule is therefore needed for inter-
generational equity. Maximin might look like a candidate but if
we assume that saving is a cost to the generation who carry it
out and a benefit to subsequent ones this would entail no saving
at all, because the first generation would have to act in conflict
with maximin if *they* were to save, and each successive generation is then a 'first generation' in the sense that it comes into a
situation where there has been no prior saving. I shall discuss
Rawls's solution briefly in another context (Chapter 12) but in
the meantime nothing is lost if we overlook this complication.

The next point is: what are 'social and economic inequalities'? Economic inequality is a complex matter since there are
many ways in which people may have different claims on
resources: private property invested in various ways to bring
in dividends, capital gains or fixed interest, rights in a pension
or to certain benefits payable in specified contingencies, income
from employment, perquisites of all kinds, and so on. Aggregat-

ing these to produce a distribution of income requires many
conceptual decisions about which there can be disagreement.[1]
Moreover, even if we could decide in principle what the distribution of either income or wealth was among individuals at a
point in time this would be very inadequate as a measure of
'real' inequality for at least two reasons. First, we should not
wish to say that a society in which everyone had the same
income at the same age but in which income differed greatly
according to age was as unequal as one with the same distribution of income at a single point in time but in which the inequality reflected gross differences in the lifetime expected
earnings of different people. (A parallel point could be made
about the distribution of the stock of wealth.) And, second, the
appropriate unit (especially for measuring inequalities of
wealth but also for income) is not individuals but families, so
that one would wish to say that a man with a lot of dependants
was less well off (and so were the dependants) than a man in
receipt of the same net income with few or no dependants. How
wide the net should be cast in aggregating wealth or income and
attributing it to a single family, however, is determined by the
way the money is actually spread around, which depends partly
on the legal framework, partly on social norms and partly on
individual decisions.

Notice, incidentally, that in drawing attention to things one
would wish to take into account when talking about economic
inequalities I am not intending to have anything to do with the
idea put by some recent writers that saying something is an
'inequality' is to claim that it is unjustified, so that 'differences'
which the speaker holds to be justified are not to be described
as 'inequalities'. It is obvious that Rawls wishes to specify the
condition under which *inequalities* are *justified* so we could
make no sense of his discussion if we were to understand by
an inequality an unjustified difference. I entirely share the view
implicit in such a discussion that it must be possible to talk
about the existence of equality or inequality as a separate
question from the question whether a given distribution of

1. See for example in relation to Britain: R. M. Titmuss, *Income Distribution and Social Change: A Study in Criticism* (London: Allen and Unwin,
1962) and A. B. Atkinson, *Unequal Shares: Wealth in Britain* (London: Allen
Lane, The Penguin Press, 1972).

income or wealth is or is not ethically justifiable. My present point is simply that the criteria of an equal distribution are not as obvious and straightforward as one might unreflectingly suppose.

However, having stated some of the problems inherent in establishing a measure of economic equality I shall not discuss them further here. It is, I think, sufficiently clear for the purposes of a critical analysis of Rawls's theory what in general terms is meant by the notion of an economic inequality. It would be even easier to unbalance this book by entering into a long discussion of the concept of equality and inequality of power, for this raises a lot of very intractable problems which lie at the heart of social and political theory. I shall postpone such an analysis until another and more suitable occasion. From the contexts in which Rawls speaks of inequalities of power it seems fairly evident that he is thinking of hierarchical authority relationships, that is to say relations covered by a norm to the effect that one party commands and the other obeys. I am well aware that this is not a simple relationship and that much more analytical development would be needed before one could even ask intelligibly how to fit in bargaining power (such as trade unions hold in relation to employers or business organizations in relation to government) or formal instruments of control over those with power such as the right to elect them. But I shall resolutely ignore them.

A little more must be said, though, about social inequality. It will be recalled that Rawls spoke of 'social and economic inequalities' but he at no time says what is meant by 'social inequality'. We have to start right at the beginning here, then, and ask the preliminary question what is the nature of the good whose distribution is the subject-matter of attributions of social equality or inequality to a situation or a whole society. The usual interpretation would, I suppose, be that the good is that of 'social status'. But it will be recalled from the discussion of primary goods that only two things were mentioned as providing the content for the second principle: wealth and power. Status, the remaining member of the now standard trilogy, is conspicuous by its absence. Rawls does not deal with the omission explicitly but as I understand his position it is that in a just society there would not be any distinctions of social status so the question how it should be distributed simply would not arise. The point is not that it would exist and be distributed equally but that there would be no such thing as social status, and thus nothing to distribute.

When we say that distinctions of social status exist in a society we mean, I suggest, something as follows. Any transaction in the society (doing business, greeting, etc.) may be modified or determined in its form according to the relative positions of the parties on criteria of social honour. These criteria range from legally or quasi-legally fixed status-group attributes, such as nobility/commonership or gradations of ritual purity, through less rigid but systemic features as occupation, on to indices such as accent, bearing or dress.[2] The kinds of behaviour which exhibit differential social status may take many forms. The extreme forms of deferential behaviour—ritual abasement or formal acts of homage—tend to go with rigid status divisions.[3] At the other end of the scale the differences in address and treatment produced in a modern industrial society by different modes of dress or speech may be quite subtle. But there is no need to trespass further into Goffman territory. I hope that I have said enough to explain what is meant here by 'social status'.

Rawls's view, as far as I can see, is as follows. Differences in wealth and power are justified in two ways (a) as incentives to attract candidates into certain jobs and then to encourage them to do them well and (b) as facilities for providing required services to the rest of the society.[4] Inequalities of status are

2. It should perhaps be explained that 'race' or 'colour' do not appear in the list because they may occur at any point in it, depending on the society. The antebellum South of the U.S.A. and contemporary South Africa use a 'racial' criterion to define legal status-groups. In other societies (such as Britain and the U.S.A.) the closest approximation to the situation would seem to be the second category, while in societies like those of the West Indies it would appear to work more like the third, a dark skin setting up expectations of (for example) low occupational position which may be rebutted.

3. I should make it clear that I am talking about status distinctions within a society at large. Within hierarchic organizations such as churches and armies different statuses may be rigidly defined and the elaboration of deference rituals carried far.

4. Thus, power is attached to a position not as bait only but because it is considered necessary to have someone in a position to wield that amount of power. In the case of wealth the argument would be that a certain style

necessary neither as incentives nor as means to the fulfilment of socially desirable tasks. Therefore inequality of status will not occur in a just society.

Rawls sweeps away a great many real problems when he says that, to avoid an index-number difficulty, he will assume that wealth and power always go together. Similarly if he assumes (as he appears to) that social status would always go with wealth and power he makes it look more like a gratuitous additional advantage. We have to think of it both as a possible addition to them and as a possible alternative to them. And it appears to me that arguments of some plausibility can be constructed parallel to those Rawls accepts for the justice of inequalities in wealth and power tending to show that inequalities of social status may also be justified within his theory.

If we take the first line of justification for inequality, in terms of incentives, we could suggest that people might be paid in the coinage of status as an alternative (perhaps a partial alternative) to being given wealth or power. It is possible, indeed, that there may be those whose services are valuable, even vital, but whose exertions cannot be secured by anything except status. For 'the man who has everything' the only remaining gratification may be to receive more deference. The desire for wealth may be satiated (provided it is wanted for what it can buy and not as an end in itself) and, although power is much more addictive, it is not necessarily a good bargain for a society to offer more power to someone already powerful rather than offer him more status.

Taking up the second line of justification for inequality, we may notice that conservatives have often argued that a structure of differential social status is functional for a society as a whole. The argument is that inequalities of power are unavoidable, but they are made more acceptable not less if they are paralleled by inequalities of status. A man would sooner, it is suggested, take orders from one he regards as his social

of life is necessary in order to do certain jobs. This conception of power and wealth as socially valuable facilities rather than means to the gratification of the holder, with its conservative Parsonian overtones, is not put forward explicitly by Rawls. But it is required as an underpinning by some of the arguments in favour of inequality of wealth that he says could be accepted within the theory given appropriate factual premises. And within limits the idea that inequalities of power are necessary seems unavoidable.

superior than one he regards as his equal. Not surprisingly, Samuel Johnson put the point forcefully:

JOHNSON, '. . . Now, Sir, that respect for authority is much more easily granted to a man whose father has had it, than to an upstart, and so Society is more easily supported.' BOSWELL. 'Perhaps, Sir, it might be done by the respect belonging to the office, as among the Romans, where the dress, the *toga*, inspired reverence.' JOHNSON. 'Why, Sir, we know very little about the Romans. But, surely, it is much easier to respect a man who has always had respect, than to respect a man who we know was last year no better than ourselves, and will be no better next year. In republicks there is not a respect for authority, but a fear of power.'[5]

As any novel about the Second World War suggests, the British army still at that time took the view that the primary requisite for 'officer material' was the habit of effortless superiority to be acquired only in public schools.

A parallel argument can be constructed, with perhaps less confidence, in relation to wealth. If, as Rawls suggests, there have to be inequalities of wealth, it may be that those who are not specially rewarded would find the inequality less galling in a society which encouraged the belief that the wealthy were socially superior to them, rather than people 'no better than themselves'.

It may be, and this I am not at all sure about, that Rawls would wish to reject inequality of status by invoking the primary good of 'self-respect', which he regards as having a very high priority among the different primary goods. As I pointed out, he does not consider whether gross inequalities of wealth or power might not be subversive of self-respect but perhaps status would be thought to cut rather nearer the bone. The point here is, as I have already mentioned, that Rawls treats it either as an analytic truth or as a universally valid generalization that self-respect requires social reinforcement. The question is how far in that case equality of self-respect depends on the absence of differential social status. It may be that Rawls believes it does. If so I think he would be mistaken. Even if we allow it to be true that each person's self-respect requires that some 'significant others' respect him (or at least that they should have done so in the formative period of his life) this

5. Boswell, *Life of Johnson* (London: Oxford University Press, 1970), p. 464.

does not require the absence of society-wide status inequality. The phenomenon of groups with very low status in a society at large fostering a high degree of self-respect among their members is not even uncommon, let alone nonexistent. Often the claim is made within the group to a superiority which does not require validation from outside: the members of the group are possessed of the one true religious doctrine, for example.

It would appear, then, that alongside wealth and power, status should be included as a primary good with whose distribution the second principle is concerned. However, although this qualification should be borne in mind I shall not keep harping on it. In any case the other point that needs to be raised is discussed by Rawls using only the primary good of wealth as an illustration and for convenience I shall follow him in this. This point is simply: how do we define the 'worst off' whose position is to be improved as much as possible?

This may seem a simple enough matter. The worst-off member of a society is the person with the fewest of the primary goods covered by the second principle and the object decreed by the first part of the second principle is that whoever has the least should have as much as it is feasible for him to have. But this is not how Rawls intends 'worst-off' to be understood. 'Another thing to bear in mind is that when principles mention persons, or require that everyone gain from an inequality, the reference is to representative persons holding the various social positions, or offices, or whatever, established by the basic structure. Thus in applying the second principle I assume that it is possible to assign an expectation of well-being to representative individuals holding these positions.' (Page 64.) It should be noticed that this applies to both principles and not only the second one, but Rawls discusses it almost exclusively in relation to the first part of the second principle and I shall follow him in this. As he says of this principle, it 'selects one representative for a special role. The serious difficulty is how to define the least fortunate group.' (Page 98.)

To this 'serious difficulty' Rawls devotes a little under one page out of six hundred, and his treatment of it can only be described as offhand. When we add that his 'solutions' such as they are rob the principle of whatever egalitarian content it might appear on first sight to have, it will surely be clear that my characterization of Rawls as an unreconstructed Gladstonian liberal is not far off the mark. Rawls gives two alternatives for the definition of the position of the 'worst-off representative man' and says either will do, the choice resting on grounds of practical applicability.

One possibility is to choose a particular social position, say that of the unskilled worker, and then to count as the least advantaged all those with the average income and wealth of this group, or less. The expectation of the lowest representative man is defined as the average taken over this whole class. Another alternative is a definition solely in terms of relative income and wealth with no reference to social position. Thus all persons with less than half of the median income and wealth may be taken as the least advantaged segment. . . . I assume therefore that the persons in the original position understand the difference principle to be defined in one of these ways. They interpret it from the first as a limited aggregative principle and assess it as such in comparison with other standards. It is not as if they agreed to think of the least advantaged as literally the worst off individual and then in order to make this criterion work adopted in practice some form of averaging. (Page 98.)

Surely not since Locke's theory of property have such potentially radical premises been used as the foundation for something so little disturbing to the *status quo*! The parallel is indeed fairly precise. For Locke drops the idea that everyone has property in what he mixes his labour with in the light of the observation that the poorest labourer in England lives better than a king in America. But at least he had the decency to make the claim for the *poorest* labourer—not the average.

What I think gives this passage a particular air of having been found in a drawer of John Stuart Mill's or Herbert Spencer's desk is that it is now widely accepted that in the advanced industrial societies the problem of poverty cannot be tackled by raising the average income of all unskilled workers or increasing any other broadly-drawn average. It is now thought that the chief sources of poverty are such things as having children, being sick or unemployed for a long period, being old or being disabled. There are also certain pockets of low pay such as (in many countries, including industrial ones) agriculture and jobs done almost exclusively by women. These causes of poverty could remain untackled while either of

Rawls's indices for the 'worst-off representative man' were maximized. Indeed, in the absence of specially directed and vigorous efforts by the state, there seems to be a tendency for those hit by these sources of poverty to fall ever further behind as the society's average wealth increases.

We are now left only with the second part of the second principle, which states that social and economic inequalities are to be arranged so that they are 'attached to offices and positions open to all under conditions of fair equality of opportunity' (page 302). The intepretation of this principle does not raise any great difficulties and I shall not rehearse Rawls's discussion of it in any detail. 'Open to all' means formally open in the sense that nobody is debarred from applying: the 'career open to talent'. 'Under conditions of fair equality of opportunity' means that, subject to the continued existence of the family with its present possibilities for giving differential advantages, the maximum amount is to be done to achieve a condition of meritocracy (merit, it will be recalled, having been defined by Michael Young in *The Rise of the Meritocracy* as I.Q. + effort). It need hardly be said that we know enough now about the effects of different family backgrounds to be aware that Rawls's proviso is virtually a nullifying condition!

I have now completed my statement of the two principles of justice. But it will be convenient to add here as an addendum to the present chapter a statement of the relations between and within them. I have already said, in informal terms, that the first principle has absolute priority over the second, but I have only mentioned in passing what this means. In the terms I shall use from now on, the two principles are in a lexicographical relationship.[6] 'Lexicographic' ordering is that used in dictionaries. Of any two words the one with a first letter earlier in the alphabet is put first. Only if two words have the same first letter does the second letter affect the ordering, and then the tie on the first letter is broken by putting the one whose second letter comes earlier in the alphabet ahead of the other. And so on. Similarly, if two principles are lexicographically

6. Rawls uses the same word which has now acquired the status of a technical term, but shortens it to 'lexical' on the grounds that 'lexicographic' is too cumbersome. It is difficult to avoid the wish that this sudden passion for brevity might have gripped Rawls in some more effective way than to shorten the total length of the book by perhaps two lines.

ordered one situation is ranked ahead of another if it comes higher on the first principle irrespective of how they fare relatively to each other on the second principle. Only if two situations are equally good when the first principle is applied will the second principle be brought into play to break the tie. Thus, when Rawls says that the first principle of justice is lexicographically prior to the second this means that if one situation is better than another on the first principle, by however small a margin, it is to be preferred to that other situation even if the other situation is enormously better on the basis of the second principle.

Now it is possible, at least theoretically, that by giving up some of their fundamental liberties men are sufficiently compensated by the resulting social and economic gains. . . . Imagine . . . that men forego certain political rights when the economic returns are significant and their capacity to influence the course of policy by the exercise of these rights would be marginal in any case. It is this kind of exchange which the two principles as stated rule out; being arranged in serial order they do not permit exchanges between basic liberties and economic and social gains. The serial ordering of principles expresses an underlying preference among primary social goods. When this preference is rational so likewise is the choice of these principles in this order. (Pages 62–3.)

Whether or not it is rational I shall try to determine later. I shall also at that point discuss a proviso which Rawls adds, namely that the lexicographic ordering holds only for societies with a high enough level of 'civilization' or economic development. According to Rawls, where there is lacking some (unspecified) minimum level of development it is permissible to sacrifice the rights covered by the first principle in the pursuit of wealth (see pages 542–3).

There is also a lexicographical relation between the two parts of the second principle. The second part has priority over the first. In other words, no potential gain to the wealth or power of the worst-off representative man can compensate for the smallest extra falling away from the implementation of open competition. I shall discuss the plausibility of this relationship too in the course of examining the derivation of the two principles from the 'original position'. This will be the task of the next six chapters.

6

THE DERIVATION OF
PRIMARY GOODS

RAWLS does not discuss in any detail to what extent different parts of his theory may be accepted and rejected independently of one another. He does mention that one might have different 'original positions' and derive from them different principles, and also that one might find the two principles of justice acceptable even if one rejects the idea of deriving them from an original position. But these are only two of a multitude of possibilities. The full set is I think contained in this decision tree:

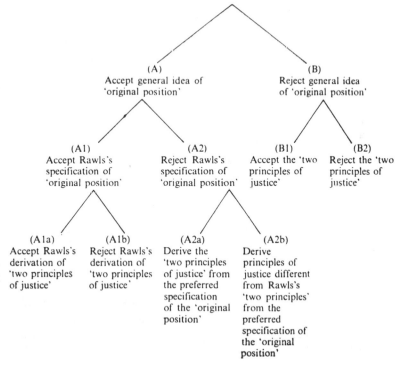

Clearly, the right-hand side of the decision tree could be subdivided almost indefinitely, to reflect the fact that there are many alternatives to approaching morality through an original position, each of which can be developed in any number of different ways. For the present purpose, however, all we need is what (B1) and (B2) give, that wherever you start from you either finish up with Rawls's two principles of justice or you finish up with something else. The left-hand side is more fully analysed here. By saying that someone accepts the general doctrine of the original position I mean simply that he believes it to be a useful way of proceeding to ask what choices people would make under conditions to some degree artificial. But one might agree with this while wanting to conceive the original position differently from Rawls, or one might conceive it in the same way but wish to argue that different principles would be chosen.

The question to be posed in this and the following five chapters comes some way down the left-hand side of the decision tree. It is this: given that we are at (A1), do we want to move to (A1a) or to (A1b)? Although this question covers only one corner of the tree, it is obviously of major significance for the coherence of Rawls's arguments. It is also a question which has occasioned a good deal of controversy on the basis of the papers published before *A Theory of Justice* and it is of some interest to see how far Rawls has succeeded in meeting criticisms of earlier versions. From time to time in the course of this discussion I shall operate at other points in the decision tree, but it will be apparent that a book many times the size of this one would be required to cover systematically all the questions that could be raised.

I shall begin, repeating my order of exposition, by asking whether the parties in the original position would, as Rawls maintains, agree that the principles to govern their social arrangements should be defined in terms of primary goods. In asking this I shall for now leave aside the question whether the primary goods that Rawls lists have the properties that he claims for them, the better to concentrate on the question whether it would be rational to agree on *any* principles defined in terms of primary goods, rather than degrees of want-satisfaction, pleasure, mental and physical well-being, or what have you. It is important here to make sure that we get the question straight, for Rawls's discussion in fact tends to confuse the issue. He writes that

the clearest basis for interpersonal comparisons is in terms of primary goods, things that every rational person is presumed to want whatever else he wants. . . . Of course, the utilitarian could concede this objection [that want-satisfaction is difficult to measure], accept the account of primary goods, and then define his principle in terms of the relevant indexes of these. This involves a major change in the theory which I shall not follow up. (Pages 174–5.)

It must be recognized here that no utilitarian has ever suggested that laws and institutional rules should themselves be specified in terms of want-satisfaction. The claim of utilitarianism is that want-satisfaction provides the ultimate criterion in terms of which laws and institutional rules are to be judged. For utilitarians to take primary goods of the kind Rawls describes as surrogates for want-satisfaction would not therefore be an innovation, but is something they have always done. Bentham, in his lifelong activity of proposing codified laws, constitutional codes and so on, defined them in terms of rights and liberties, wealth and power—not 'utility'. Similarly egalitarians propose policies for the distribution of primary goods in the hope of producing a rough equality of satisfactions but not policies for the distribution of satisfaction as such. How could they?

The distinction lies at a different point. Rawls's 'two principles of justice' are final in the form laid down, that is, defined in terms of primary goods. But a utilitarian, or anyone else whose ultimate principles are expressed in terms of want-satisfaction, well-being, etc., proceeds in the way Rawls says (as if it were an innovation) that he might conceivably do. That is to say he proposes distributions of primary goods with an eye to their effects on the thing whose distribution he regards as ultimately important. This eye Rawls would have us keep closed. 'Justice as fairness . . . does not look behind the use which persons make of the rights and opportunities available to them in order to measure, much less to maximize, the satisfactions they achieve.' (Page 94.)

The case against this refusal to go behind primary goods can most vividly be presented by saying that it rules out any extra provision for those with special needs. The concept of 'need' exists precisely as a device for grafting considerations germane to want-satisfaction onto definitions of rights defined in terms of primary goods. For Rawls a pound is a pound is a pound. Whether some people need more pounds to get to the same place as others is irrelevant. The result of this dogma is to prevent anyone from being able to claim that because of special handicaps or disadvantages he needs more income than other people to achieve the same (or less) satisfaction. Thus we rule out special allowances for the blind or otherwise handicapped, or to the sick and infirm, or to pregnant women, designed to offset the special expenses associated with those conditions. For all such individuated benefits, if we are not allowed to look behind the distribution of income to personal circumstances which give the same income a different significance for different people, must simply look like arbitrary inequalities. There is no particular reason to suppose that most of these payments would go to those worst off in financial terms, so the invocation of the maximin principle, however interpreted, does not get us anywhere.

I do not see any good reason why the parties in Rawls's original position should choose to define their principles in terms of primary goods. And it is interesting to notice that some of the ideas about the requirements of rationality which are put forward by Rawls himself would seem to tell against anything which would prevent claims based on special need from being given recognition in public policy. According to Rawls, rational men, when choosing the principles that will govern the most important social institutions, will adopt a conservative attitude. By this is meant that they will react asymmetrically to the prospects of large gains and large losses, being much more concerned to avoid catastrophe than to have a chance of enormous gains. This is employed by Rawls as an argument in favour of the maximin criterion, which concentrates emphasis on the bottom rather than the top or even the average of the distribution.

But we can surely out-Rawls Rawls here. For the same considerations suggest that it would be irrational to assent to a way of defining principles that would prevent the recognition of claims based on special need. What, after all, could be a more devastating prospect than that of being seriously ill in a society without a free health service or disabled in a society without a humane system of poor relief? Take a society at the level of affluence of Victorian England, and read the harrowing accounts of the lives of disabled people in Mayhew's *London Labour and the London Poor* if you want to see the case for taking special needs into account. Anyone in the original position would surely insist that any society at that economic level or a higher one should have a publicly organized system for dealing with special needs. Herbert Spencer or William Graham Sumner might celebrate the virtues of the 'struggle for existence' and argue on pseudo-Darwinian grounds the advantages to 'society' of eliminating the 'unfit' by starvation and hardship, but even if (as Rawls suggests) the people in the original position accepted the social science of the time, they would not be impressed by this because of their concern to avoid very bad outcomes which they might be unfortunate enough to incur themselves.

Before we move on, it ought to be mentioned that, although Rawls has hardly anything to say about social policy (a significantly low priority when one considers that for many working-class people in industrial societies 'fairness' is virtually entirely comprised in the provisions of the welfare state) he does say at one point in passing that 'the government guarantees a social minimum either by family allowances and special payments for sickness and employment [sic], or more systematically by such devices as a graded income supplement (a so-called negative income tax)'. (Page 275.) The question here, however, is not what Rawls himself believes should be done but what follows from his theory. A negative income tax is something that would fit his theory to the extent that it does not make allowance for special needs. But it is not an alternative to the provision of extra resources for those who need more in order to compensate for extra costs, like the sick. Family allowances I have not yet mentioned because children, although they can be regarded as additional costs to those who bring them up, can alternatively be regarded as separate entities for the application of the maximin criterion. As with negative income tax, the compatibility of family allowances with the theory turns on the interpretation given to the maximin criterion. The interpretation proposed by Rawls would not seem to require them. As we have seen, he suggests two possible interpretations of the 'worst off'. One is the average unskilled manual worker and the other a person with half the median income. In both cases one presumably takes a standard family of the relevant kind, with two and a half children. Family allowances would not therefore affect the minimum so defined, and negative income tax would probably affect only those who were below the level defined by Rawls for his 'minimum' so it would not make any difference to the 'worst-off' representative man on his own conception of 'worst-off'.

Let us, in order to proceed with our discussion, waive these objections to the definition of principles in a form which allows no reference to anything behind primary goods. Suppose that the formulation of principles in terms of primary goods is accepted. We can still ask whether Rawls has correctly stated which things *are* primary goods and also whether the priority relations that he asserts to stand between the various primary goods really hold. It should also be observed that, although it is most convenient to conduct the discussion on the assumption that the role of primary goods is accepted, most of the discussion would be equally relevant if we amended Rawls's theory to allow for an appeal behind primary goods. For the question of the absolute and relative values of wealth, power and freedom remains an important question of political philosophy. All that depends on the issue just discussed is how the criteria for their distribution should be defined.

7

THE DERIVATION OF
THE PRIORITY OF LIBERTY

THE question of absolute value—whether Rawls's primary goods are good things at all—I shall postpone because it gets us into deep waters. For now let us assume that they have some value—that more of them is better than less—and consider Rawls's proposed priority relations. For although, as I shall suggest, it is possible to argue that these things do not have value, the view that they do have some is a quite normal one. It is much less clear than might appear on the surface what precisely Rawls wishes to say about the priority of liberty. The main effort in this chapter will therefore be an attempt to develop two alternative systematic reconstructions of Rawls's statements on the subject. Having done that I shall ask whether either view of the 'priority of liberty' would be accepted in the original position, making use where relevant of earlier discussions.

Let us begin by recalling Rawls's final statement of the priority relationship: '*First Priority Rule* (The Priority of Liberty). The principles of justice are to be ranked in lexical order and therefore liberty can be restricted only for the sake of liberty.' (Page 302.) In the section 'The Priority of Liberty Defined' (§39) we can find the point spelt out a little more fully: 'By the priority of liberty I mean the precedence of the principle of equal liberty over the second principle of justice. The two principles are in lexical order, and therefore the claims of liberty are to be satisfied first. Until this is achieved no other principle comes into play.' (Page 244.)

The implication of lexicographic ordering between two principles is that, as between two situations, the smallest superiority on the first principle outweighs any amount of superiority on the second principle and that the smallest amount of improvement on the first principle is worth sacrificing any amount of loss on the second principle. The contrast is with a 'pluralistic' relation, in which each of the principles would be ascribed a weight and choices made between alternative situations by 'trading-off' gains and losses on the two principles at the prescribed rate of exchange. Rawls makes it clear that it is precisely such 'trading-off' that he wishes to reject.

Now it is possible, at least theoretically, that by giving up some of their fundamental liberties men are sufficiently compensated by the resulting social and economic gains. . . . Imagine . . . that men forego certain political rights when the economic returns are significant and their capacity to influence policy by the exercise of these rights would be marginal in any case. It is this kind of case which the principles as stated rule out; being in serial order they do not permit exchanges between basic liberties and economic gains. (Pages 62–3.)

This might be called Rawls's official doctrine, and it is the one he refers to most of the time in the book. It is, as stated, so outlandishly extreme that it is scarcely worth devoting any space to its discussion. It can be accepted only if wealth is assigned a value that is literally infinitesimally small in relation to liberty, so that it would be judged worth dropping from general affluence to general poverty in order to score a minute gain on the 'liberty' criterion, if such a choice were presented to a society. In the end, however, Rawls does not defend this official view. Indeed, even when introducing the notion of lexicographic ordering, in §8 ('The Priority Problem') he writes: 'While it seems clear that, in general, a lexical order cannot be strictly correct, it may be an illuminating approximation under certain special though significant conditions (§82).' (Page 45.) Almost five hundred pages later, near the end of the book, we finally arrive at §82, which is entitled 'The Grounds for the Priority of Liberty'. Here at last we get a chance to see what is covered by the qualification 'certain special though significant conditions' and it is Rawls's discussion in this section of the book to which I shall address myself in the remainder of this chapter.

Actually, it is not clear what exactly Rawls does want to say here, though there is no doubt that he wishes to arrive at a particular conclusion, namely that it is rational for a society to pursue increased wealth up to some point even at the expense of the equal basic liberties guaranteed by the first principle. The most easily comprehensible statement of his position makes it appear that he intends to relax the lexicographic priority of the first principle so that at low levels of economic development a degree of 'pluralistic' trading-off between liberty and wealth can be allowed. This interpretation is especially suggested by the talk of 'marginal significance' in the following passage:

Now the basis for the priority of liberty is roughly as follows: as the conditions of civilization improve, the marginal significance for our good of further economic and social advantages diminishes relative to the interests of liberty, which become stronger as the conditions for the exercise of the equal freedoms are more fully exercised. Beyond some point it becomes and then remains irrational from the standpoint of the original position to acknowledge a lesser liberty for the sake of greater material means and amenities of office. (Page 542.)

Now, the most convenient way of discussing trading-off relationships between two goods is to represent them graphically by means of indifference curves. (Rawls does this himself to illustrate his discussion of 'pluralism' on page 37.) Figure 1 is an attempt to draw the indifference map implied by the passage just quoted. Several points about the construction may be noted. First, the axes. Along the vertical axis are amounts of 'liberty', increasing with distance from the origin in the bottom left hand corner. This dimension is shown as having an upper bound, indicating that it makes sense to think of the maximum possible equal liberty being achieved within a society.[1] Position

1. Indeed, Rawls attaches some importance to the idea that it is conceivable, and even quite feasible, that a society should achieve a position in which the 'equal liberty' criterion is completely satisfied. In his preliminary discussion of lexicographic ordering he says that 'unless the earlier principles [in the lexicographically related series] have but a limited application and establish definite requirements which can be fulfilled, later principles will never come into play. Thus the principle of equal liberty can assume a prior position since it may, let us suppose, be satisfied. Whereas if the principle of utility were first, it would render otiose all subsequent criteria.' (Page 44.) As a statement about the necessary and sufficient conditions for the lower-ranking criteria in a lexicographically related series to come into play this is in fact incorrect. The complete satisfaction of the first principle might be consistent with only one choice and thus leave no room for the second

along the horizontal axis indicates the level of the society's wealth. It is not conceived as having any definite upper limit. In this connection it is worth remembering that wealth is treated within Rawls's theory as a primary good in itself; it is

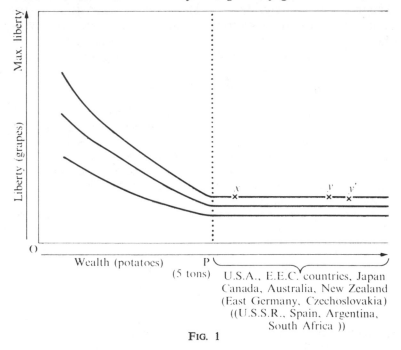

FIG. 1

thus the kind of thing measured by indices of Gross National Product rather than something that might be captured by a more sophisticated conception of economic welfare explicitly relating production to the satisfaction of human needs.

It must be recognized that we are here dealing in terms of the aggregate national income of the society in question. It would not be valid to assume that two societies with the same average *per capita* income must have their 'worst-off representative

principle to operate. Conversely, the imperfect satisfaction of the first principle is quite consistent with the second principle's coming into play, provided there is more than one way of satisfying the first principle to exactly the same degree and no feasible way of satisfying it more than that degree. But the present point is that Rawls clearly does believe that the principle of equal liberty can be completely satisfied.

man' at the same economic level. Even if in both societies the governments were faithful and conscientious followers of the rule that the position of the 'worst-off representative man' should be raised as far as possible there could presumably be technical and cultural factors which would make the same average compatible with a variety of very different minima. The reader may wonder whether Rawls should not have pitched his discussion of priorities in terms of the affluence of the 'worst-off representative man' rather than the overall level of wealth of the society—and with good reason—but I am at present simply trying to expound the position as Rawls sets it out.

Let us now consider the indifference curves. An indifference curve connects points representing different combinations of the two goods which are equally desirable. Following what would appear to be the implications of Rawls's reference to the diminishing marginal significance of wealth as the society has more of it, we show a family of indifference curves with a downward slope at low levels of wealth to indicate that at these levels it is worth trading some liberty for an increase in wealth. These curves are shown as gradually flattening out as they move to the right until at the point P they all become horizontal. This means that beyond P no gain in wealth compensates for a reduction in the degree to which the 'equal liberty' criterion is satisfied. P is thus the 'point [at which] it becomes irrational from the standpoint of the original position to acknowledge a lesser liberty for the sake of greater material means and amenities of office.' (Page 542.)

We cannot attach a quantitive figure, in terms of G.N.P. *per capita*, to the point P on the basis of Rawls's discussion. But we can in a rough and ready way use the names of contemporary societies as surrogates. It is clear from the whole drift of Rawls's discussion, here and at other places in the book, that he thinks some contemporary societies are past the point P, so that he is talking about an actual rather than a hypothetical situation.[2] Since he is an American and often uses terms such as 'we' in connection with social choices, it is safe to put the U.S.A. to the right; and if the U.S.A. then presumably also the other countries listed without brackets. The countries in a single pair

2. 'For the most part I shall assume that the requisite circumstances for the serial [lexicographic] order obtain.' (Page 152.)

of brackets would seem plausible candidates while those in double brackets raise questions of diverse kinds which it would have been nice to have Rawls's ruling on. We cannot on the basis of anything Rawls says assign actual positions to countries in relation to the point P or attach any definite date to the time when those that are to the right of P passed it.

There are three technical points which are worth making here. First, it is surely clear that it is misleading to describe the relation between the two principles as one of lexicographic priority. The set of indifference curves for any good which must be consumed in a fixed time will presumably reach a point eventually where they are parallel with the axis, indicating that further amounts of the good are not wanted at any price; but would it be helpful to say money had lexicographic priority over the good? Indeed, if the axes represented two goods, both of which had the characteristic that additional amounts beyond some quantity were of no value one would be obliged to say, on Rawls's criterion, that each was lexicographically prior to the other, which would be rather absurd. To make our ideas more definite let us in Figure 1 replace liberty with grapes and wealth with potatoes, and provide that the goods cannot be sold if they are not used. Point P might then be (as shown in Figure 1) five tons of potatoes. Rawls would have us say that, given we have five tons of potatoes, grapes have a lexicographic priority. There are surely better ways of describing the position.

Second, we should note that Rawls says things that are inconsistent with his statement that beyond a certain point it is not worth sacrificing liberty for increased wealth. As Figure 1 shows, the implications of being able to say that when we have five tons of potatoes no offer of further potatoes will induce us to part with a single grape is that once we have five tons of potatoes any more potatoes are totally without value. But Rawls remarks, in the paragraph following that just quoted: 'To be sure, it is not the case that when the priority of liberty holds, all material wants are satisfied. Rather these desires are not so compelling as to make it rational for the persons in the original position to agree to satisfy them by accepting a less than equal freedom.' (Page 543.) But if wants for material goods, even if not 'compelling', still have some value in fulfilment (at least for some people, we had better add) this would not seem to fit in with the indifference curves representing the society's collective preferences being parallel to the axis; it suggests a shallow slope. Rawls might reply to this that the problem arises because we can only represent the priority relation graphically by a line parallel to the axis, whereas the implication of a lexicographic ordering is that the second principle acts as a tie-breaker. This, however, is a point of trivial significance in the present context. It means that, in Figure 1, point x is less good than point y, instead of being just as good, but it still means that point x is better than a point y', which we may define as a point an infinitesimal distance below y. In other terms, it means that if we get ten thousand grapes anyway we would sooner have ten tons of potatoes than five tons, but we would prefer five tons of potatoes and ten thousand grapes to ten tons of potatoes and nine thousand nine hundred and ninety-nine grapes. This is surely not giving economic goods the kind of value which Rawls implies that they still have at the point where the priority of liberty becomes absolute. There is thus, it would appear, an unresolved contradiction between Rawls's claim that beyond a certain point an additional increment of wealth is not worth the sacrifice of the smallest amount of liberty for the society as a whole and his statement that at this point there are still un-satisfied material wants (presumably especially among the worst-off) which are merely less 'compelling' than at lower levels of wealth. The second of these statements seems to me a good deal more sensible than the first and if it is accepted then the lexicographic priority of the first principle understood in this sense has to be dropped altogether.

A third, and more intriguing, point is that this artificial and dubious notion of a threshold beyond which liberty has abso-lute priority does not have the logical consequences that Rawls seems to suppose it has. He writes as though, once the priority of liberty (in this sense) has been established, it follows im-mediately that as a society grew more prosperous it would at some stage reach the threshold (the point P) at which liberty has priority; at that point and not before the society would pursue liberty only. But the optimal path cannot be deduced in this way from a knowledge of the indifference curves only. We also need to know the shapes of the curves representing the sets of feasible combinations open to the society. When we fill out the picture in this way we find that the conclusions which Rawls wants to arrive at about the optimal choice path can be derived in an alternative way without the strained assumptions about the shapes of indifference curves which he has proposed.

To explain these points, let us go back to the grapes and potatoes. If we want to know how many grapes and how many potatoes someone will choose we need to know not just what combinations he likes equally well but also what combinations are available to him. His 'feasible set' can be represented graphically by a line connecting all combinations of grapes and potatoes available (a 'feasibility curve'). There may be a fixed price relating the two, so that (say) one potato has to be given up for each six grapes, in which case the line would be straight. This is the normal situation confronting someone whose purchases are small in relation to the market. Grapes are, say, six a penny and potatoes one a penny, so if someone has twenty pence he can buy 120 grapes and no potatoes, 114 grapes and one potato, and so on. Another point is that if he had, say, twice as much money the relative prices facing him would still be the same. Graphically, this means that the lines are not only straight but parallel to one another (Figure 2). Even under these conditions, the proportions of grapes and potatoes bought may well vary according to the person's income. Thus, in Figure 2, the highest attainable indifference curve with the lower feasible set of combinations (FC1) available is IC1, while that attainable on twice the income (FC2) is IC2; and if we compare the two choices made (C1 and C2) we can observe that the proportion of potatoes to grapes (given by the ratio of horizontal to vertical broken lines) is higher in the first case than the second. By adding other intermediate lines and finding on each the point at which an indifference curve is tangential, we can construct a line which shows how the person's pattern of purchases would change as he acquired more income. This is the line shown as the 'optimal path of expenditure' in Figure 2.

If we are thinking not of the situation facing a single consumer but the set of feasible alternatives open to a society, the lines cannot be expected in general to be straight or parallel. Thus, to take a hackneyed instance, suppose that the choice is between producing guns or butter domestically. It would be most odd if the transfer of resources from one to the other gave a constant exchange rate between them. A bulging line representing the combinations available, like FC1 in Figure 3 would be much more plausible. This would signify that at each point the larger the proportion of total resources that has already been put into producing guns the fewer the additional guns

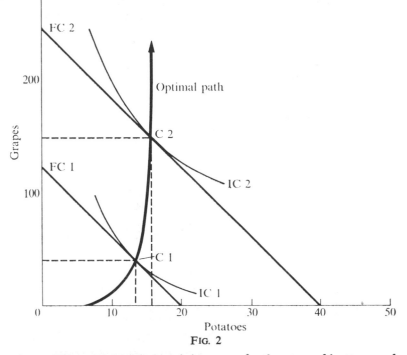

FIG. 2

that will be obtainable by giving up a further ton of butter, and *vice versa*. The position of FC2 in relation to FC1 has the significance that if the country had a higher national income the transformation rate between guns and butter would change so as to make guns relatively cheaper in terms of butter, or, to put it the other way round, so as to require more guns to be given up for each additional ton of butter. As the society develops economically it moves to feasibility curves successively further from the origin.

At each stage of economic development, corresponding to a curve showing the feasible combinations of guns and butter, the

particular combination that ought to be chosen is the one that
touches the highest attainable indifference curve. This 'ought'
is a mere implication of the meaning of feasible sets and indifference curves: it says that the purposes of the person or
group of people to whom the indifference curves belong will be
furthered by their choosing in that way. Any set of indifference
curves for the distribution of a society's resources reflects some
judgement by somebody or some group about what they would

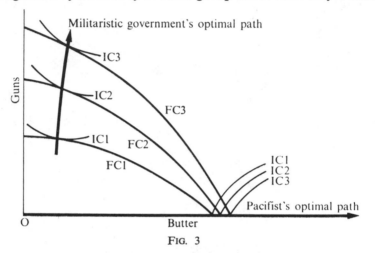

FIG. 3

like to see—whether they be men in a Rawlsian original position, individuals making recommendations which they hope
others will agree with or governments formulating their policies. Naturally the shapes of the indifference curves will differ
radically if the premises underlying them do, and so therefore
will the optimal paths. Thus, in Figure 3 there are entered two
families of hypothetical indifference curves. One is attributed to
an absolute pacifist and has the characteristic that he thinks that
x amount of butter (for all values of x) plus some guns is worse
than x with no guns, and the more guns the worse it is. The
optimal path lies along the 'butter' axis. The other family of
curves is attributed to a militaristic government which considers
that some minimum amount of butter is necessary to avoid a
degree of discontent that would lead to its overthrow but that
above that level guns are much more important than butter.
The optimal path is almost parallel with the 'guns' axis.

In applying this kind of analysis to Rawls's two kinds of goods let us start by simply assuming that some simple set of curves represents the feasible sets of combinations of freedom and wealth of a society with progressively more area of choice, that is to say, a society which can have at each stage more equal freedom and the same level of wealth or more wealth and the same degree of equal freedom. The feasibility curves are num-

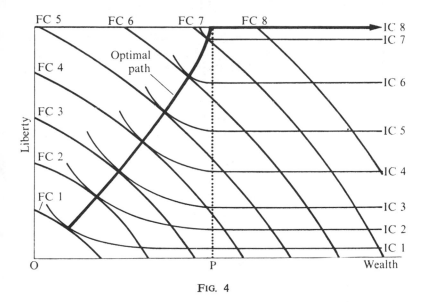

FIG. 4

bered one to eight in Figure 4, each representing a successive stage of economic development. It may be worth dwelling a little on this interpretation of the feasibility curves. In the case of guns and butter it is fairly clear that the feasibility curves represented stages of economic development in that a curve further from the origin denotes a greater productive capacity than one nearer to it. The greater productive capacity can be used to have more guns and the same amount of butter, more butter and the same amount of guns, or a smaller increase in the amount of both at once. It may be less apparent that we can call a shift from one feasibility curve to another one further from the origin 'economic development' when the two axes represent G.N.P. and liberty. But it is clear that between two states represented by one feasibility curve and another further from the origin there is a difference in productive capacity because in the second state it would be possible to have the same amount of liberty and a greater G.N.P.

The point is that we are here assuming feasibility curves of the usual shape. This entails that at each point on the feasibility frontier (i.e. the feasibility curve representing its currently available feasible set of combinations) the society is faced with a choice between more liberty and less G.N.P. or more G.N.P. and less liberty. In other words, we are assuming, in drawing the feasibility curves this way, that any increase in liberty is productively inefficient. (I shall query this assumption a little later.) Therefore, if a society follows a path from one feasibility curve to another by having more liberty and the same amount of G.N.P. it is foregoing the increased production of goods and services that it might have had and in effect buying liberty instead. We can put it another way. Since the shape of the feasibility curves implies that liberty is productively inefficient there must have been some net capital investment, some newly discovered natural resource, or some improvement in technology between the two situations so as to permit the *same* level of production to continue in spite of the increase in liberty.

On these lines showing successive feasible combinations for the society we superimpose indifference curves of the shape suggested by Rawls, and the result is as in Figure 4. The optimal path for the society can now be constructed, since we know that the optimal point at any time lies where the feasibility curve touches the highest attainable indifference curve. What cannot be read off from Figure 4, or even guessed at, is the speed with which the society moves along its optimal path, assuming that it does in fact follow it. The wealth measured along the horizontal axis may be either consumed or invested, but the proportion going to each is not shown. Other things being equal, the rate at which the society moves outward from the origin through successive feasibility curves depends on the amount set aside for investment. And this in turn can be regarded as determined at any time by the size of the G.N.P. and the proportion of it going to investment. Thus, if we take a society on a a certain feasibility curve and ask how fast it will get to another one further from the origin we san say (1) that for a given investment rate (i.e. proportion of G.N.P. invested) it will move faster the more it has chosen G.N.P. at the expense of liberty and (2) that for a given G.N.P. it will move faster the higher the proportion invested. In order to prevent things getting out of hand completely I shall (except in one footnote later in the chapter) sweep this complication under the carpet, thereby following the example set by Rawls himself, by assuming that a 'just savings rate' is to be applied at each stage of economic development.

It may be most helpful to think of the decision-process as running in a different order from that presented above. We might think of the first decision to be taken as the decision how much to invest in further economic development. Then when the claims of the present and the future have been adjusted, setting aside as a first call on the feasible combinations a certain amount of production for investment, the decision can be made between two competing claims for the current use of the society's remaining productive potential: consumption of goods and services and the alternative of liberty, which in the present context might be thought of as a special intangible kind of consumer good.

There are two interesting points about the optimal path in Figure 4. The first is that, although we have followed Rawls's prescription for the indifference curves, the optimal path does not become vertical, showing the pursuit of liberty at any cost in increase of wealth. This is likely to be the case since in general we would expect the location of the tangency to be to the left of the point at which the indifference curves became horizontal. Whenever this is so it has the implication that the society does not get to the point P on the wealth axis until it has reached the maximum freedom. If one thinks about this, it is a reasonable enough result of the shapes imposed on the indifference curves by Rawls, for if the curves become horizontal at a certain point we should expect them (in the absence of any argument to the contrary) to be nearly horizontal as they approach this point. We can put the same point non-geometrically as follows: if the relative value of one of the two goods falls to nothing when one has a certain amount of it, it would generally be irrational to get even close to the point where it becomes valueless until one has as much as possible of the other.

The second point to notice is that in the end the horizontal indifference curves which Rawls has worked so hard to establish are not crucial to the optimal path. We could, in Figure 4, make the indifference curves slope down gently beyond the point P instead of being flat without making the optimal path change its course one iota, so long as we left the points of tangency to the left of the point P in the same place. So if we take it that Rawls is concerned to show that, at some level of wealth, freedom should be pursued as the only goal, and further wealth not pursued at all if it has any cost whatever in terms of freedom, we have to say that his indifference curves are far from guaranteeing him this result.

I also suggested earlier that the kind of result Rawls wants can be arrived at without these indifference curve assumptions, and this I shall now explain. Instead of taking funny indifference curves and standard feasibility curves, I propose that we do the reverse: let us take indifference curves of ordinary shape but try to make an argument for unusually shaped feasibility curves. This I think can be done quite plausibly since there are good reasons for suggesting that freedom and G.N.P. are not related in the same way as guns and butter. The relation I wish to argue for is one of the kind shown in Figure 5, where, as before, we have eight lines representing increasing ranges of choice, that is to say increasing levels of 'civilization' or 'development'. The significance of their shapes is that countries at a low level of development (those with feasible sets shown by lines near the origin) can obtain a fairly large increase in wealth by sacrificing a given amount of liberty, but that as countries become more developed the amount of extra wealth that can be gained by moving along the feasibility curve so as to sacrifice that same amount of equal liberty becomes less. As the economy becomes more sophisticated, the need for managerial initiative and for predictability in the operation of the law becomes more pressing, while at the same time the working population becomes more accustomed to the routines of industrialism and the traumatic social changes of the initial stages are not paralleled in scale or severity by those which accompany increasing economic development.

As I have drawn the curves, several have at least a section which is vertical or outward sloping. This implies that a certain minimum of liberty is either neutral with respect to the production of material goods or actually conducive to it. The further from the origin the line showing feasible combinations of the two the more marked this compatibility between them becomes. This seems to me to correspond with common sense,

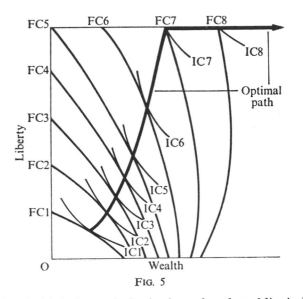

FIG. 5

and in fact I think the societies in the unbracketed list in Figure 1 are in a position where a reduction in personal liberty would have little or no effect on productivity. If this is so then it means there is no need for choice (and indeed no possibility of a choice) between wealth and liberty. This is reflected in the shape of the optimal path, which quickly rises to near the maximum amount of liberty, though the bulging shape of the feasibility curves prevents it from hitting the maximum until the line is outward-sloping almost all the way. Recall that this is all with standard indifference curves, which are drawn so as to make both wealth *and* freedom worth little when there is a great deal of them already. The fact that the optimal path rapidly approaches the maximum amount of freedom simply reflects the fact that very little has to be sacrificed in order to get there.

The argument may be less heroic than that of Rawls but it seems to me a much more plausible way of getting the kind of answer he wants.

Indeed, I am myself more confident of the vertical and backward-sloping parts of the feasibility curves than the rest. Is it really true, in particular, that countries at a low level of development have to (or, to put it another way, can if they wish) have more wealth by sacrificing personal liberty? The idea that there is a trade-off is a common one, better established among social scientists than some of the 'social science' Rawls imports into the original position as unquestioned generalizations. But how is the trade-off supposed to work? Why should liberty interfere with production or production with liberty?

Perhaps the answer to this question is that the only way to get more than a certain amount of material production out of a society at a given stage of development is to make people work much harder than they want to, by enslaving them or in other ways using extreme coercion, and this is obviously incompatible with allowing full equal liberty. However, it should be noticed that a society's optimal path would not get onto this part of its feasibility curve except where the social indifference curves were imposed by a minority backed by coercive powers sufficient to overcome the reluctance of the rest of the society to follow this path. A society would never get into this position if its collective indifference curve were based on, for example, the classical utilitarian criterion, since *ex hypothesi* it is a position strongly unwanted by the bulk of the members of the society.[3]

3. There are, I am afraid, a good many complications here which I can only glance at. One is that the incompatibility of a certain level of production with freedom (at a given stage of economic development) may depend on the distribution of the benefits of the increased production. If the additional wealth created goes into the pockets of a minority, coercion may well be needed; whereas the bulk of the population would work harder if the benefits were to accrue to them. I do not however believe that cases are non-existent of societies with a traditional pattern of life whose members would prefer to do without increased production even if the benefits of their own efforts went to themselves. Another complication is that the 'production versus liberty' question cannot be separated from the 'consumption versus investment' question since the second pair are both calls on production. The coercion by the government to hold down protest and counter-moves against high production (given the state of development) may be in the interests not of consumption by either a current majority or

The worry motivating Rawls's theory of the (conditionally) absolute priority of liberty is that people might prefer more wealth to more liberty even when they were not desperately poor. But what I am suggesting is that to the extent that they want wealth they probably cannot get more by giving up liberty; there is only the possibility of getting increased material production at the expense of liberty to the extent that they don't want the extra material production (at the price that has to be paid in extra work). It is not therefore necessary for Rawls to make such strenuous efforts to rule out the rationality of selling one's birthright for a mess of pottage. For if I am right the only way of getting more pottage by selling one's birthright would be by choosing to be coerced into working harder than one thought worth while; and this it would clearly be irrational to do. If I am not right, and it would be possible to get a great increase of production with little more work by making, say, a small sacrifice of equal liberty then I do not see why it would be irrational to accept this trade. If the feasibility curve were almost horizontal in its upper part, Rawls's stipulation of horizontal indifference curves beyond the point P would affect the optimal path. (This is the only exception to my earlier statement that it would not make any difference if they sloped down at a shallow angle to the right of the point P.) At the point P the society would be obliged to pursue only increased liberty even though (*ex hypothesi*) each increment of liberty involved forgoing a great deal of additional wealth. But it does not appear to me that Rawls ever argues persuasively that the men in the original position would be rational to bind themselves in advance to making this decision if the world happens to pose them with this particular choice. (Notice again that if they were *sure* it would not be possible to gain a great amount of material goods for a small amount of liberty there would be no practical difference between horizontal and shallowly sloping indifference curves anyway.) Presumably Rawls would wish to suggest that this extreme preference for liberty over economic goods is underwritten by the 'Aristotelian principle' but this seems

a current minority but by future generations, as in Britain from say 1780 to 1850 or the U.S.S.R. under Stalin's five year plans. It is a nice question whether a government committed to the Rawlsian 'just savings rate' would be justified in suppressing liberty in order to impose the 'just savings rate' on an unwilling population.

inconsistent with the admission that at point P further economic goods are still valued. And in any case I have already argued that the 'Aristotelian principle' is not very plausible.

I should now like to offer an alternative interpretation of what Rawls may have in mind when he speaks of the 'conditional priority of liberty'. The advantages of this interpretation are first that it produces (if the units are chosen suitably) exactly the right shape of optimal path; and, second, that it makes sense of certain ideas to which Rawls seems to attach importance since he repeats them in two different places in the book. Its disadvantage is that it involves the creation of a new key variable, 'effective liberty' or 'exercised liberty', on the basis of only the most sketchy guidance from the text about its significance and behaviour. But the idea is one that has certainly been put forward by other liberals, so it may be of interest to work it out briefly here; and in any case it seems very difficult to understand the passages I shall quote unless something of the kind is attributed to Rawls.

On pages 151–2 Rawls says that:

roughly, the idea underlying this [lexicographic] ordering is that if the parties assume that their basic liberties can be effectively exercised, they will not exchange a lesser liberty for an improvement in economic well-being. It is only when social conditions do not allow the effective establishment of these rights that one can concede their limitation; and these restrictions can be granted only to the extent that they are necessary to prepare the way for a free society. The denial of equal liberty can be defended only if it is necessary to raise the level of civilization so that in due course these freedoms can be enjoyed. Thus in adopting a serial order we are in effect making a special assumption in the original position, namely, that the parties know that the conditions of their society, whatever they are, admit the effective realization of the equal liberties.

And on page 542, in the paragraph immediately preceding the one quoted from earlier which is said to provide 'the basis for the priority of liberty' we get an almost word for word repeat of this passage, now referred to as containing 'the intuitive idea behind the precedence of liberty'. There is however one new clause which, if taken seriously, would introduce a major modification. Rawls now says that 'if the persons in the original position assume that their basic liberties can be effectively exercised, they will not exchange a lesser liberty for an improvement in their economic well-being, *at least not once a certain level of wealth has been attained'*. The italicized clause suggests that until some (unspecified) level of wealth has been reached it would be rational to give up liberty for economic improvement even if the level reached was already such as to allow the basic liberties to be effectively exercised.

Let us leave aside this clause and stick to the elements common to the two widely separated passages. These are: (1) that the basic liberties covered by the first principle of justice acquire value only to the extent that they can be 'effectively exercised', 'effectively established' or 'effectively realized' (all three expressions are used), (2) that the conditions of 'effectiveness' are material ones and (3) that wealth has value only insofar as it provides the material conditions for the 'effective exercise' (etc.) of the 'basic liberties' (except in a lexicographically secondary way). Unfortunately, Rawls nowhere spells out the political philosophy implied by items (1) and (2) above. But presumably the idea is that basic liberty cannot be 'enjoyed' (another expression Rawls uses in the same context) unless people reach some necessary level of wealth. Why this should be so is not at all clear to me. Is there anything in the *material* situation of, say, a group of nomadic Bedouin eking a bare subsistence from the desert or a population of poor peasant cultivators which would prevent them from being able to use personal liberty? Perhaps, however, Rawls has in mind that the material conditions should make it possible for children to be given some form of education (including at least literacy) and that adults should have enough leisure to read and talk, and so on. This would relate him to those nineteenth-century liberals who wished to emphasize the social preconditions for the enjoyment of freedom.[4]

I shall not pursue further the question what is the nature of the connection between basic liberty, effective liberty and wealth. I shall now ask what the *form* of the connection is, and hope that the answer to this does not depend too critically on the answer to the other question. Taking two extreme cases, it

4. For a sympathetic reconstruction of such a view see W. L. Weinstein, 'The Concept of Liberty in Nineteenth-Century English Political Thought', *Political Studies*, xiii (1965), 145–62.

would seem reasonable to say that a zero level of basic liberty accompanied by any amount of wealth gives a zero level of effective liberty; and similarly that any amount of basic liberty accompanied by no wealth at all would give a zero level of effective liberty, since the people involved would soon die of starvation. We also know from Rawls that beyond some amount further increments of wealth do not increase the effective liberty produced by any given amount of basic liberty.

The simplest way of putting these points together would be to say that no amount of basic liberty, however great, produces any effective liberty unless it is combined with some fixed minimum level of wealth; and that beyond this minimum level of wealth no increment of wealth adds to the effective liberty produced by any given amount of basic liberty. This, however, would be very crude. A more complex (though still relatively simple) way of representing the situation which also satisfies the conditions set out would be to say that we have a multiplicative relationship, the amount of effective liberty being the product of the amount of basic liberty and the amount of wealth, subject to the limitation that beyond some point further wealth does not increase the product any further.

In thinking about the relations among the three variables it is once again important to remember that these variables are defined in aggregate terms to refer to a whole society. Presumably the increase in aggregate effective liberty brought about by an increase in aggregate wealth and the limit on the possible increase would be the reflection of some functional relationship at the level of the individual person between wealth and basic liberty on the one hand and effective liberty on the other. Once again, the distribution of income among persons and any change in it would be crucial in determining the actual effects of an increase in national income upon the aggregate effective liberty, as would be the precise nature of a functional relationship at the individual level. It seems fairly obvious that a multiplicative relation with a cut-off is likely to be too simple to capture the joint effects of these two factors at the aggregate level but it is complex enough to show the general idea.[5]

5. A more sophisticated aggregate relationship would show increments of wealth having a decreasing marginal value in producing effective liberty when combined with any given amount of basic liberty. This is more reasonable for two reasons. Firstly, the individual relationship would surely be

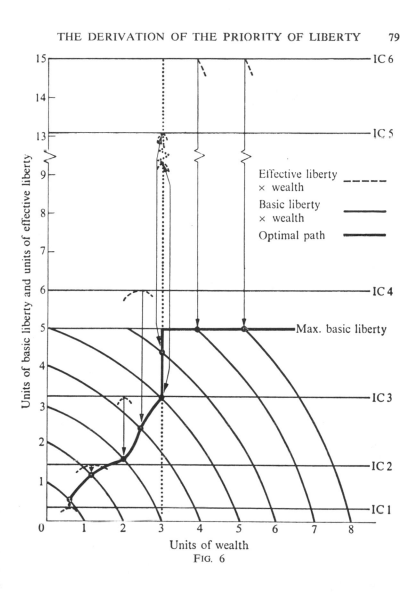

FIG. 6

most plausibly conceived in this form, and so even with equal incomes the aggregate relation would take this form too. And, secondly, the diminishing marginal effectiveness of aggregate income would be enhanced by an unequal distribution of income, provided the distribution were roughly pyramidal in shape; under these conditions, indeed, there would be *aggregate* diminishing marginal effectiveness if the *individual*-level functional relation were a multiplicative one with a cut-off or even if it took the simple all-or-nothing form we first considered as a possible aggregate relationship.

This idea is illustrated in Figure 6. Feasibility curves of a standard shape are drawn to connect basic liberty with wealth. But it is also assumed that to each combination of these two there corresponds a single value on the new variable of effective liberty. In Figure 6, we take it that at no units of wealth effective liberty is always zero; at one unit of wealth, the number of units of effective liberty is the same as the number of units of basic liberty; at two units of wealth, the number of units of effective liberty is twice the number of units of basic liberty; and at three units it is three times. But further increases of wealth beyond three units do not produce any greater increase in the value of effective liberty for any given level of basic liberty. The number of units of effective liberty stays at three times the number of units of basic liberty.

On Figure 6 I have plotted the curves relating effective liberty and wealth, and these are shown with dashed lines. The scale for units of effective liberty on the vertical axis is the same as that used for units of basic liberty. It will be seen that, as before, we are assuming that there is an upper bound to the possible amount of basic liberty. Since this is set here at five units and the most by which units of basic liberty can be multiplied to give units of effective liberty is a factor of three, it follows that there is a maximum of effective liberty at fifteen units.

Now, of course, the optimal path for a society is not given until we also have the shape of the indifference curves specified. But this is governed by point (3) in our statement of assumptions above, which read: 'wealth has value only inasfar as it provides the material conditions for the 'effective exercise' (etc.) of the 'basic liberties' (except in a lexicographically secondary way). Following this we can immediately deduce that the indifference curves relating 'effective liberty' to wealth will run parallel to the wealth axis. We can add the lexicographic relation between the two by saying that of two positions of the same indifference curve (i.e. equally good in terms of 'effective liberty') that one is to be preferred which is further along the wealth axis. The indifference curves at the points of tangency have been drawn in on Figure 6. Each point of tangency is of course at the maximum level of 'effective liberty' provided by the corresponding feasibility curve relating basic liberty and wealth.

By dropping a perpendicular from each point of tangency to its corresponding point on the feasibility curve we can show the optimal mixes of basic liberty and wealth, and connecting up these points gives us the society's optimal path. It will be seen that this follows a line gratifyingly close to that which Rawls would appear to want. At low levels of economic development the society pursues both more wealth and more basic liberty. Then its path hits the point (3 units) at which further increases in wealth do not multiply the units of basic liberty by any larger factor, and at this point the optimal path becomes vertical, signifying that the society pursues only further basic liberty. It continues on this vertical path until the maximum amount of basic liberty is reached, whereupon the optimal path stays at the upper bound of basic liberty and moves along it in the direction of greater wealth.

The precise location of the optimal path in the example depends, of course, on all the details of that example: the shape of the feasibility curves and the relative sizes of the multiplying factor, its maximum and the maximum number of units of basic liberty attainable. But the essential point of the example is that horizontal indifference curves for effective liberty are compatible with the pursuit first of wealth and basic liberty and then basic liberty only until the maximum is reached; and this feature of the optimal path can be reproduced over a wide range of variation in the specification of the factors that determine it. This is enough to show that the second interpretation of Rawls put forward in this chapter is at any rate internally consistent.

I have so far in this chapter addressed myself less to the derivation of the priority of liberty than to the question what the doctrine of the priority of liberty actually is, since this obviously has to be settled first. I have taken the essential point to be the claim that once some minimal level of economic development has been achieved by a society (that is, once it gets to a feasible set of combinations of wealth and liberty which lies some distance from the origin) the pursuit of further equal liberty has absolute priority over the pursuit of increased wealth (that is, the optimal path become parallel to the 'liberty' axis). And I suggested two ways in which Rawls may wish to arrive at this conclusion. The first, and most obvious, involved the relationship between indifference curves and feasibility curves for liberty and wealth. I took Rawls to be suggesting that at a certain point all the indifference curves become parallel to the 'wealth' axis and pointed out that this did not in general result in the optimal path ever being parallel to the 'liberty' axis. However, this construction of the indifference curves does guarantee that at the point where the indifference curves become horizontal the optimal path will lie at the maximum possible equal liberty. But I suggested that in the (in my view highly unlikely) circumstance that this would involve the sacrifice of vast amounts of wealth in order to obtain the last scrap of equal liberty the people in the original position have not been proved by Rawls to be rational in insisting in advance on going for liberty.

The second interpretation offered involved the construction of a variable—effective liberty—which I assumed was the sole value to be pursued, and I showed how it could plausibly be related to wealth and basic liberty in such a way that the optimal path through successive feasibility curves would follow a mixture of the two for some time and then pursue the increase of basic liberty until the maximum level of these was reached. If we ask whether this kind of objective can successfully be attributed to the people in the original position we are still, I think, thrown back on the question whether or not we can swallow the 'Aristotelian principle'. Unless we can, I do not see how we can agree that the people in the 'original position' would be rational to commit themselves to the position that wealth is of value only to the extent that it increases 'effective liberty' rather than as a contribution to convenience, comfort or self-indulgence.

8

THE DERIVATION OF
EQUAL OPPORTUNITY

IN this chapter and the next two I shall discuss the derivation
of the double-barrelled second principle of justice. The first
part of the principle is the maximin criterion for the distribution of wealth and power and the second is the requirement of
'fair equality of opportunity' in the competition for advantageous offices and positions. In spite of its apparently smaller
significance, the second part is, as we have seen, given lexicographic priority over the first. But why is it there at all? If it is
justified only as a means to the satisfaction of the maximin
criterion it is redundant: we could easily imagine a dozen subordinate principles corollary to the maximin criterion at least
as plausible as this one. Rawls does make a good deal of play
with the idea that the equal-opportunity provision will help to
satisfy the maximin criterion. Thus, whenever he discusses the
objection that maximin is consistent with gross inequality he
makes the point that equality of opportunity would hold down
the rewards required to get people into positions requiring
special abilities or training by making the field as large as possible. No doubt it is true that restriction of access has always
been a way in which professional groups have increased their
advantages, but all this shows is that a society which accepted
the maximin criterion would adopt a policy of open competition
for jobs. It does not provide any reason for erecting 'fair
equality of opportunity' into an independent principle.

Rawls sees this problem clearly enough in *A Theory of
Justice*, though he did not, I think, regard it as a problem when
the two-part principle first appeared in 'Justice as Fairness'.

However, his attempts to justify the independent and prior status of equal opportunity seem to me to have a rather desperately *ad hoc* air about them. As so often when in a tight corner, Rawls reaches for the 'Aristotelian principle', thus giving rise to the curious result that one of the two parts of the principle dealing with the distribution of wealth and power is actually justified as an independent criterion by its alleged relation to the non-interest primary goods. This is one of the things I had in mind when I said that the reader who sets himself to comprehend the precise relation between the elements in Rawls's theory should not be surprised if he notices steam coming out of his ears.

There is one passage which explicitly puts forward the case for the independence of the second part of the second principle.

The reasons for requiring open positions are not solely, or even primarily, those of efficiency. I have not maintained that offices must be open if in fact everyone is to benefit from [?such—B.B.] an arrangement. For it may be possible to improve everyone's situation by assigning certain powers and benefits to positions despite the fact that certain groups are excluded from them. Although access is restricted, perhaps these offices can still attract superior talent and encourage better performance. But the principle of open positions forbids this. It expresses the conviction that if some places were not open on a basis fair to all, those kept out would be right in feeling unjustly treated even though they benefited from the greater efforts of those who were allowed to hold them. They would be justified in their complaint not only because they were excluded from certain rewards of office such as wealth and privilege, but because they were debarred from experiencing the realization of self which comes from a skillful and devoted exercise of social duties. They would be deprived of one of the main forms of human good. (Page 84.)

Rawls does not, it seems to me, put the contingency to be discussed in a very apt way. The case he describes as one where restriction of competition could be justified in terms of the maximin criterion does not appear to be so. For if some members of the excluded group would have got jobs instead of the least well-placed candidates who actually got them, the exclusion is operating so that a given degree of incentive is failing to produce the best qualified candidates that it might. (If none of the excluded group would have got a job in fair competition, their exclusion obviously makes no difference anyway.)

What you would have to do in order to justify a limitation of access to posts as an actual contribution to the satisfaction of the maximin criterion would be to argue that even if the restriction produced slightly worse winners abstractly considered, there was some factor which would make them work better together and thus produce better overall results. Thus, the exclusion of women from some jobs is claimed to produce a better working relationship, or fewer distractions, and racial discrimination in employment is similarly sometimes justified as a contribution to harmony. American medical schools, with their notorious quota on Jewish entrants, are said to reflect the belief among the luminaries of the profession that too many Jews would spoil the *ésprit de corps* and introduce a sordid note of competition into the gentlemanly (and lucrative) scaling of fees, which is alleged to be beneficial to the public. Rawls does in fact discuss arguments of this general type later, when he mentions Burkean notions of the advantage to a society of having a privileged class with special access to political office. His discussion of the possibility that this might be justified within his theory is very obscure. Among other things he says that it would be justified if 'the attempt to eliminate these inequalities would so interfere with the social system and the operations of the economy that in the long run anyway the opportunities of the disadvantaged would be even more limited' (page 301). This seems to suggest that the lexicographic priority of the second part of the second principle over the first part is as shaky and conditional as the priority claimed for the first principle over the second.

However, let us ignore this piece of backsliding and examine the rest of the passage which was quoted above. The key sentences are the last two. But it is important in assessing their force to remember that feelings of injustice based on 'intuitive' notions like desert have no place in Rawls's theory. The only 'sense of justice' that can be acknowledged is one which accepts the principles deducible from the original position, and the question here is which principles *are* deducible. It is no use, in other words, bringing in our substantive moral idea that the best qualified person 'ought' to get the job because he has an intrinsically stronger claim to it. In a Rawlsian society claims based on desert can mean only 'Given the rules I should have got so-and-so'. As he himself correctly says, considerations of desert cannot be a basis for the rules themselves, but the question at present is precisely what rules should be adopted with respect to competition for jobs. The question, then, is whether the parties in the 'original position' would be rational in giving equal opportunity lexicographic priority over the maximin criterion for distributing power and wealth. The justification is in terms of the good that holding office does to the office-holder, not the good that the office-holder may do for society. This strikes me as quixotic. I am reminded by it of the occasion when an Oxbridge Fellow with certain personal problems was appointed to a chair at a new university. The story went that the Vice-Chancellor became tired of getting the response, when he boasted of his new acquisition, 'Yes, it'll be so good for him'.

If we ruthlessly eliminate from our minds, as those in the original position are supposed to have done, any hankering after substantive justice conceived in terms of desert, we must surely say that inasfar as holding offices of responsibility is fun this is a lucky by-product, not the point of having them. And if self-development is really the point, it is not particularly likely to be maximized (still less maximinimized) by fair competition for offices. If 'the office makes the man' it should perhaps have a chance to build up otherwise insignificant people. Those with talent will probably do all right anyway.

9

THE DERIVATION OF
THE MAXIMIN CRITERION

I SHALL assume from here on that the second part of the second principle can be dismissed as an independent criterion, and this, at one point at least, as I suggested, seems to be Rawls's own view. This leaves us with the first part of the second principle. I have already discussed Rawls's proposed interpretation of the worst-off whose lot is to be made as advantageous as possible. But his arguments for the maximin criterion, if valid at all, would appear to me to lead to a far more bracing interpretation of 'worst off'. The main question about the derivation, however, turns on the rationality of committing oneself to a principle which ties the evaluation of a social system entirely to how well-off the 'worst-off representative man' is, however he is defined. Can it be rational to espouse a principle which throws away so much *prima facie* relevant information, such as the average *per capita* income, the degree of dispersion round the mean, the distance between top and bottom and so on?

In 'Justice as Fairness', Rawls put forward an argument for a maximin criterion which, if it had been valid, would have been decisive. It was not, however, valid; and this is acknowledged in *A Theory of Justice*. The curious thing is that, having withdrawn the original premises, he retains the same conclusion but substitutes new premises from which the conclusion may be derived.

Rawls argued in 'Justice as Fairness' that the men in an informal approximation of the 'original position', would 'propose principles of a general kind' and that these principles will express the conditions in accordance with which each is the least unwilling to have his interests limited in the design of practices, given the competing interest of the others, on the supposition that interests of others will be limited likewise. *The restrictions which would so arise might be thought of as those a person would keep in mind if he were designing a practice in which his enemy were to assign him his place.*[1]

Some years ago I set out the case against accepting this argument in the following terms:

'Now, if the sentence I have italicized is right, it must be allowed that Rawls's deduction works. A man whose place is to be assigned him by his enemy will obviously concentrate on designing the system of distributions so that the worst-off position will be as pleasant as possible. He knows that he can, and must, concentrate on this and ignore everything else, because he knows for certain that, whatever the worst-off position is, he will be occupying it. But our hypothetical principle-choosers are *not* going to be assigned their positions by their enemy. They know in fact that the allocation of places will depend (in proportions that they do not know) on personal characteristics and on luck. And since they do not at the moment remember what personal characteristics they have, they can simply regard positions as allocated by a random process.

'Now the question is, if you know that outcomes are determined by a random process (or, more generally, by a process which is not directed at giving you personally one outcome rather than another) is it rational to behave as if the outcome were going to be determined by the wishes of your enemy? This is the vexed problem of decision-making under conditions of uncertainty. Rawls's solution has been put forward often as the maximin criterion: "maximin" simply refers to the fact that it prescribes the choice which *maximizes* the *minimum* pay-off. In other words, the decision-maker looks at the possible consequences of each alternative to discover the worst possible outcome that each could produce. For each alternative he asks: if everything went wrong, how catastrophic would it be? And he then picks up the alternative which gives him the smallest losses if everything goes wrong. Clearly this is a play-safe

1. Laslett and Runciman, *Philosophy* ..., Second Series, pp. 138–9. My italics.

strategy, a conservative strategy. Does it make sense as a universal response to uncertainty?

'Let us consider a simple example. Either it will rain today or the sun will shine; and I can either take my raincoat or leave it at home. If the sun shines and I have left my raincoat, I shall be very pleased; on the other hand, if I leave my raincoat and it rains, I shall be very annoyed. If I take my raincoat and it rains, I shall be fairly pleased in that I am at least suitably clad, though less pleased than the combination of sun and no raincoat would make me; if the sun shines when I take my raincoat, I shall be somewhat annoyed, though less annoyed than I would would be at having to walk through the rain without a raincoat.

'The maximin criterion dictates that I take my raincoat: the worst that can happen is that the sun will shine; and this is less annoying than the worst thing that can happen if I leave my raincoat behind, namely get wet. This would obviously be the right plan if I were convinced that there was a Weather Man who took a malicious pleasure in thwarting me. But if I thought that "someone up there likes me" and was striving to make me as happy as possible, I would be more sensible to adopt a maximax policy: instead of choosing the best of the worst outcomes I would go for the best of the best outcomes. In the present case, this would entail that I leave my raincoat behind and trust in providence to make the sun shine, for my most pleasant outcome consists of the combination of no raincoat and the sun shining.

'Suppose, however, that I don't believe that my decision about taking a raincoat or not will have any effect on whether it rains or whether the sun shines. How should I decide then which to do? The natural answer would seem to be that I should try to guess how likely it is to rain and should act accordingly. If there is a fair chance of its raining, I take my coat; if I think the chance of rain is very remote, I leave it behind. Exactly how likely rain has to be before it is worth taking my coat depends on the relative pleasantness and unpleasantness of the four possible outcomes and my taste for risk-taking. Fortunately, there is no need for the present purpose to go into details. The essential point is that almost anyone would think it sensible to go out without a raincoat if the probability of rainfall is below *some* level, but on the maximin criterion one would always take a raincoat if there was any chance of rain at all, however remote. The conclusion to be drawn is, I suggest, that it is not rational to follow the maximin policy except where someone *is* responding to your choices in such a way as to damage you. In other cases some sort of system for playing the percentages is more rational.'[2]

In *A Theory of Justice*, Rawls again says that 'the two principles are those a person would choose for the design of a society in which his enemy is to assign him his place' (page 152) but nullifies this as a relevant argument by adding: 'The persons in the original position do not, of course, assume that their initial place in society is decided by a malevolent opponent. As I note below, they should not reason from false premises.' (Page 153.) He begins his real argument in the book by saying that 'this analogy suggests that if the original position has been described so that it is rational for the parties to adopt the conservative attitude expressed by [the maximin] rule, a conclusive argument can indeed be constructed for these principles.' (Page 153.) Quite so, but it is hard to see that any initial plausibility has been provided by the reference to one's enemy assigning one's place.

According to Rawls there are three features of any situation which increase the rationality of a conservative approach to decision-making and he suggests that 'the original position manifests these features to the fullest possible degree, carrying them to the limit, so to speak' (page 153). At the limit, absolute conservatism is presumably in order, and hence the maximin criterion is appropriate. The three features are as follows: 'First, since the rule takes no account of the likelihood of the possible circumstances, there must be some reason for sharply discounting estimates of these probabilities.' Second, 'the person choosing has a conception of the good such that he cares very little, if anything, for what he might gain above the minimum stipend that he can, in fact, be sure of by following the maximin rule.' And third, 'the rejected alternatives have outcomes that one can hardly accept.' (All quotations from page 154.)

Let us take Rawls's three features in turn. The first says in effect that if you don't know much about the probabilities attached to the various possible outcomes of decision X, the

2. 'On Social Justice', *Oxford Review*, No. 5 (1967), 29–52, pp. 36–8.

various possible outcomes of decision *Y*, and so on, but do know what the worst possible outcome of each decision is, it is rational to take the decision which is known to have the most preferred worst outcome. Whether this is a plausible criterion for rational choice under certain peculiar kinds of uncertainty is not crucial because I think I can show that the situation in the original position is not that in which the criterion is claimed to operate. However, it may be noted that Arrow and Hurwicz have proved[3] that if a decision-maker knows all the possible outcomes of each of the alternative choices before him but has *no idea at all* of the relative probabilities of these outcomes, he will rationally take account only of the best outcome and the worst outcome that can arise from each choice. Since any outcome can occur with any probability it is obvious that any idea of maximizing expected value is out of the question in such a situation, and there is no point in looking at the outcomes between the best and the worst. But it should also be noted that this does not entail a maximin strategy. Some further argument would be required to get to the conclusion that it is rational in the circumstances to be a 'pessimist' rather than an 'optimist', and to take account only of the *worst* possible outcome.

We can pursue the question whether the original position is a situation relevant to the 'first feature' along two lines, one of which undercuts the other. Let us take the less basic point first. Rawls wishes to argue that the people in the original position do not know the probability of finding themselves in any of a number of different positions in different kinds of society (see page 155). This being so they have the choice of operating on the principle of 'insufficient reason' (i.e. the idea that in the absence of information to the contrary it is rational to assume that each separately-identifiable state is equally probable) or choosing a criterion which does not require any information about probabilities, maximin being an example of such a criterion. (See page 171.) There is no need to discuss Rawls's objections to the use of the principle of 'insufficient reason' here because if we conceive the choice to be made as one where

3. In C. F. Carter and J. L. Ford (eds.), *Uncertainty and Expectations in Economics: Essays in Honour of G. L. S. Shackle* (Oxford: Basil Blackwell, 1972) 1–11.

the parties have no information about probabilities we have to add that there are no stronger grounds for attributing to them knowledge of the range of positions available, including of course the worst-off positions. There is therefore *no* basis for rational choice in the original position.

I do not, however, want to place much weight on this refutation because I believe Rawls's whole argument at this point depends upon a monumental confusion and the refutation itself can be framed only in a way which presupposes that the confusion does not exist. What has been said so far would be relevant only if the people in the original position were choosing between different *societies*. Rawls himself in one extended passage (pages 164–75) explicitly argues as if this were a suitable way of representing the choice. The relevant passage begins: 'Imagine a situation in which a single rational individual can choose which of several societies to enter.' (Page 164.) It is then argued that, because of the uncertainties of the original position, 'if the principle of average utility is to be accepted, the parties must reason from the principle of insufficient reason' (page 171), and they would be better advised to choose the society with the highest minimum rather than that with the highest average computed on such a dubious foundation.

Now if it were true that the choice were a choice among societies, I would concede that it is at any rate arguably rational to pick the society with the highest minimum provided (a) that the alternative minima available in the different societies are known and (b) at the same time the proportions of people in each 'representative position' in each society are not known. But this is *not* the decision that the people in the original position have to make. The decision to be made is about the criterion to be used in judging the institutions of their society, whatever that society may turn out to be. In the situation where this criterion is to be used there is no extraordinary uncertainty: the situation is simply the normal one of taking decisions in an actual society. The radical uncertainty of the original position comes in the wrong place to help Rawls's argument for the maximin criterion. To have an argument he would have to say, in order to support it, that the conditions in which the chosen criterion is to be *applied* are such as to make the knowledge of probabilities impossible. Since this is a question of fact and not something that can simply be postulated, as can the degree of uncertainty in the original position, this would be a good deal more difficult to establish, nor does Rawls try to do so.[4]

It might be argued that even if in fact the world is one in which probabilities can be estimated the people in the original position do not know how uncertain the world will turn out to be, so they should specify a criterion that will be appropriate if the world turns out to be extremely uncertain. There are two possible answers to this. The first is that the body of generalizations that the people in the original position have access to can surely include the information that the world is not one in which the frequency of positions in a society in the present and under various alternative arrangements cannot be roughly estimated. The second answer is that, if the people in the original position were persuaded that the maximin criterion is an appropriate one to adopt if one is faced with the peculiar kind of uncertainty where minima are known but probabilities completely unknown, there is nothing to prevent their building a contingent statement to this effect into their criterion.

Thus, a possible two-part criterion might run as follows: (1) where an estimate can be made for each alternative (law, institution, etc.) of the level of each 'representative position' and of the proportion of the total population occupying each 'representative position', choose that alternative which maximizes the average level (that is to say the alternative which maximizes the sum obtained by multiplying the level of each 'representative position' by the number of people in it, adding the totals to

4. The same goes for a curious subsidiary argument that Rawls advances to the effect that people in the original position cannot choose a criterion with the object of maximizing expected utility because such a choice to be meaningful presupposes known tastes, whereas those in the original position do not know their tastes. (See pages 173–4.) Again, this is entirely beside the point, because all the people in the original position have to do is choose a criterion to be applied in conditions of normal knowledge. The reasoning for the criterion that average utility should be maximized, as Rawls presents it, would be that this maximizes expected utility for each individual. The cogency of this reasoning is entirely unaffected by the fact that the people in the original position do not know what their tastes are. They do (since it is a simple matter of logic) know that, whatever their tastes are, the consistent application of the 'average utility' principle will maximize their chances of satisfying them.

form a grand total and then dividing by the number of people); (2) where an estimate can be made for each alternative (law, institution, etc.) of the level of each 'representative position' but not of the proportion of the total population occupying each 'representative position', choose that alternative which maximizes the level of the lowest 'representative position'.

It is important to observe that this criterion for judging social arrangements is one that could quite happily be endorsed by a strict utilitarian. For, as I have already pointed out, the conditions obtaining in the second case are such as to make the estimation of an average level (of whatever is relevant— utility or primary goods) completely impossible. What the two-part criterion says in effect is: 'apply the utilitarian criterion (of maximizing the average) wherever you have enough information to be able to, and where you don't have this but do know the alternative minima go for the highest minimum.' A utilitarian is, obviously, someone who believes that at least in some circumstances where decisions have to be taken there is enough information to make the utilitarian criterion applicable. And where not even rough estimates of probabilities can be made one might add that it is unlikely that information will be available about the minima produced by alternative decisions either, so if the utilitarian criterion cannot be applied it is quite likely that the situation is so vague that the maximin criterion cannot be applied either.

Indeed, although Rawls suggests that the utilitarian criterion requires more information than the maximin one, it is not upon this point that he bases his rejection of utilitarianism. His discussion generally seems to take it for granted that a utilitarian judgement can be carried out in an actual society, and his objection is that the results of such a calculation may sometimes be morally repugnant. But the present point is whether, as Rawls claims, the utilitarian criterion would also be rejected in the original position, and moral repugnance cannot be called in aid by Rawls here. What I have claimed so far is that the argument for rejection which says self-interested men would not rationally choose utilitarianism because of the extreme uncertainty of the original position fails because the relevant uncertainty for the argument would have to come not when one is choosing a criterion but when one is applying it.

Perhaps I can make the point I have been putting more apparent by drawing attention to Rawls's acknowledgement that 'clearly, the maximin rule is not, in general, a suitable guide for choices under uncertainty' (page 153). This means that other criteria would be rational for use where the situation did not have the three special features mentioned by Rawls. But for this remark to make sense the relevant situation must be the situation in which the criterion is to be *applied*, not the situation in which the criterion itself is being *chosen*. For the situation in which the criterion is *chosen* is always one of complete ignorance about the answer to the question what will be the nature of the situations in which the criterion will be *applied*. This is necessarily so in as far as a general criterion for rational decision-making is intended to apply at all times and places— to stone-age men, to Roman emperors, to contemporary Bushmen or to voters in modern Western societies.

The criterion 'maximize expected utility whenever you can estimate for each alternative both the range of the possible outcomes and their probabilities of occurrence' is completely general. It is thus to be chosen in a situation of complete ignorance about the situations in which it may be applied and the specific implications for choice that it would have. If it is this kind of uncertainty which underlies the 'first feature' then such a criterion could never rationally be chosen, and Rawls's admission that the maximin criterion is a rational one to use only in very special circumstances would have to be withdrawn. If it is ever rational to use a criterion other than maximin (and Rawls says it is usually rational to do so) then it must be open to people in the original position rationally to say that *they* will use a criterion other than maximin when, having made their decision, they come out from behind the 'veil of ignorance' and apply the criterion they have chosen.

If we drop the idea that the people in the original position know about the minima obtainable and say, as it seems to me we should, that they know neither the proportions of the population in different 'representative positions' nor what the levels of 'representative positions' (including the lowest) are in the society they belong to, the circularity of Rawls's procedure at this point becomes blatantly obvious. For there is complete symmetry between the information bearing on the maximin criterion and the criterion (which is the only other one that Rawls seriously considers) of maximizing average utility. The people in the original position know that if they choose the criterion of maximizing the average each of them will gain the highest possible obtainable average individual expectation, while if they choose the criterion of maximizing the minimum each will guarantee himself the highest possible minimum individual expectation. The question then is, of course, whether it is rational to go for the highest average expectation or the highest minimum expectation. If the chooser knows his attitude to risk, the question is in principle answerable. But Rawls is clear (and rightly so) that the parties in the 'original position' cannot have any definite attitude to risk ascribed to them. He says that 'the veil of ignorance also rules out the knowledge of these inclinations: the parties do not know whether or not they have a characteristic aversion to taking chances. As far as possible the choice of a conception of justice should depend on a rational assessment of accepting risks unaffected by peculiar individual preferences for taking chances one way or the other.' (Page 172.) In the absence of a particular attitude to risks we are thus back at the basic question whether it is more rational to maximize one's average expectation or one's minimum expectation. Rawls is supposed to be trying to show that it is more rational to choose the latter, but the fact that the parties are ignorant about the range of likely averages or likely minima is part of the specification of the problem and not an argument tending towards one solution or the other. On the face of it, it would appear that Rawls has carefully removed all information (including attitude to risk) which could provide a basis for making a rational choice of a criterion. In as far as anything can be said I would suggest it might be that since the chooser does not know whether he likes risks, dislikes risks or is neutral, a version of the 'principle of insufficient reason' might lead him to act as if he were neutral. This would result in his choosing the criterion of maximizing the average. But the main thing is that Rawls establishes nothing whatever by his 'first feature'.

The other two special features which Rawls claims to be exhibited to the ultimate degree in the original position can be analysed within the framework developed so far. The 'second feature' ran as follows: 'the person choosing has a conception of the good such that he cares very little, if anything, for what he might gain above the minimum stipend that he can, in fact, be sure of by following the maximin rule.' (Page 154.) There is a preliminary point to be made. Rawls is assuming that, as a matter of psychological fact, there is a definite threshold (and the same one for everybody) up to which increments of wealth and power are valued but above which they have little or no value. On the face of it, this hardly looks at all plausible. As I observed in Chapter 7, Rawls's treatment of the priority problem would seem to entail that above some threshold wealth for a society as a whole has infinitesimal value, but I also quoted his statement contradicting this explicitly, to the effect that at the threshold there are still unfulfilled wants for economic goods. In any case, the path from a threshold for societal wealth to individual thresholds cannot simply be deduced. There are, it should also be noted, problems of internal consistency facing Rawls if he really wants to say that power and wealth above the minimum are of little or no value to anyone. For if this is so, how can the promise of gaining power and wealth above the minimum work as an incentive to get people to exert themselves in ways they would not otherwise do? That the prospect of power and wealth is an effective incentive underlies Rawls's whole assumption that differentials can be justified because they act as incentives and thus get people to do things that make even the worst-off better off than they would be in a condition of equality.

Suppose, however, that we accept the assumption that for each person there is a threshold and also that it comes in the same place for everyone. This does not lead to the deduction of a maximin criterion. Once again we can put forward the case from within what appear to be Rawls's premises or we can challenge them. If we see the question as one of choosing be-between alternative societies, the point to be made is that the people in the original position do not know what the minimum will be if they choose a society organized in accordance with the maximin criterion. Rawls's argument from the threshold effect to the maximin criterion works only if the minimum level obtainable under a maximin-satisfying organization of society happens to coincide exactly with the level at which the threshold effect operates. Pretty obviously the *a priori* probability of this being the case is exceedingly low. If the minimum obtainable is either above or below the threshold level, we cannot say without further information whether in any particular situation maximizing the minimum will be a good idea or not.

A simple illustration may help here. Suppose I am given a hundred apples to distribute among ten people, and suppose that these people have an identical Rawlsian threshold with respect to apples. If this threshold happens to lie at the level of ten apples, Rawls's argument holds. Each apple up to the tenth has a considerable value for each person and each apple after the tenth has little or no value for each person. Therefore I obviously do the best thing by giving each person ten of the apples, which is the maximin solution. (Since the total number of apples is unaffected by the way they are distributed it is also, of course, the equal solution.) But now suppose the threshold for apples lies at twelve apples. It is no longer obvious that the best thing to do is to give everyone ten; and the case against automatically following maximin when the highest minimum obtainable is (as here) below the threshold can be seen very plainly if we modify the example so as to get away from the zero-sum assumption and allow the distribution to affect the total. Suppose that we could either give everyone ten apples or nine people twelve apples and the other person nine: would it not seem quite an attractive idea to get everyone except one up to the threshold level of twelve apples even at the cost of letting the remaining one person drop from two below to three below? If the answer is given that this depends on the marginal deprivation involved in going from ten down to nine, I agree but point out that this is still getting away from the maximin approach. Since the threshold, if one does exist, is surely well above the highest minimum obtainable in any existing society this case should be regarded as the standard one.

The remaining possibility, where the threshold is below the highest minimum obtainable is, I suggest, a non-existent case. But for what it is worth it too does not make maximin an automatic choice. If the threshold, in our original example, came at a level of eight apples it is clear that the distributor should give everybody eight apples. But how should he dispose of the remaining twenty? *Ex hypothesi*, it doesn't make a great deal of difference what he does with them since they are of little or no value to anyone. But if they are of little value to some and no value to others he should surely give them to those people to whom they are of above-zero value, even if this contravenes the maximin solution. (N.B. that thresholds at the same number of apples does not entail equal marginal utilities at points either above or below the threshold—or indeed at it.)

It is important to observe here that Rawls's argument for the maximin criterion, posed in terms of primary goods rather than utility, welfare, happiness, etc. depends not only on a threshold but on its being in the same place for everyone. If five people had a threshold at eight apples and five at twelve apples the right way to distribute the hundred apples would obviously be to provide each person with the number of apples necessary to bring him to his threshold. This is of course quite contrary to Rawls's maximin criterion which he insists over and over again is to be defined in terms of primary goods: 'expectations are based upon an index of primary goods and the parties make their choice accordingly' (page 155).

This again illustrates the crucially important role played in Rawls's derivation of his 'two principles' by psychological generalizations, this time generalizations of a kind Rawls does not make explicit. For it seems clear that if we have rational self-interested people who are choosing principles in the original position and who are thus concerned to further their conception of the good, or in other words to satisfy their most important wants, we cannot suppose that they would choose a maximin criterion (or for that matter any other criterion) based upon quantities of wealth and power unless they believed everyone to have roughly the same utility-function with respect to wealth and power. It is hard to see how they could be attracted by such an approach if on the contrary they believed that a given level of, say, wealth (a) might represent grossly different levels of want-satisfaction for different people or (b) might be a point at which a certain increment of wealth would be greatly valued by some but of little or no value to others.

Rawls observes that classical utilitarians rely on what he calls 'standard assumptions': 'Thus they suppose that persons have similar utility functions which satisfy the condition of diminishing marginal utility. It follows from these stipulations that, given a fixed amount of income say, the distribution should be

equal, once we leave aside affects [sic] on future production.'
(Page 159.) He says a little later that 'the utilitarian's standard
assumptions that lead to the wanted consequences may be only
probably true, or even doubtfully so' (Page 160) but it is obvious
that Rawls merely pushes the problem back a stage by importing similarly dubious assumptions into the original position
itself.[5] Thus, when discussing the system of taxation that would
be just on his premises, he says that

the design of the distribution branch [of government] does not
presuppose the utilitarian's standard assumptions about individual
utilities. Inheritance and progressive income taxes, for example, are
not predicated on the idea that individuals have similar utility functions satisfying the diminishing marginal principle. . . . Doubts about
the shape of utility functions are irrelevant. This problem is one
for the utilitarian, not for contract theory. (Page 280.)

But the irrelevance of utility functions to the *application* of the
maximin principle in Rawls's system is bought, as we see, at
the price of making assumptions about the utility functions at
a logically prior stage. In the absence of such assumptions, the
principle, defined in terms of the distribution of wealth and
power themselves, would not have been accepted.

The more fundamental line, in relation to the 'second
feature', is to emphasize again that the parties have only to
choose criteria to be applied in a real society. They do not have
to try to apply various criteria from behind the 'veil of ignorance' and then say which one's applications they prefer. The
relevance of this to the 'second feature' is that if everyone has
the kind of similar utility function that Rawls puts forward in
order to deduce the maximin criterion (though even then as we
have seen it does not actually generate it except in the unique
situation in which the minimum is equal to the threshold) then
the principle of maximizing average utility would have the
same implications. For it would clearly be efficient in terms of
aggregate utility to get everyone up to the (identical) threshold
at which further increments of wealth and power have little or

5. I should not wish to be understood here to be accepting by default
Rawls's statement that utilitarianism requires 'standard assumptions' of
this artificial kind, and I do not believe that all utilitarians make such
assumptions. But in order to talk about one thing at a time I must defer
consideration of this point until the next chapter.

no value, if this can be done at all, rather than to let some fall below the threshold in order to allow others to rise above it.[6] Conversely, if the assumptions made by Rawls about utility functions are not correct then the people in the 'original position' will turn out to have made a bad mistake in choosing the maximin criterion in the expectation that they were correct.

Rawls's argument for the relevance of the second 'special feature' to the situation of the people in the original position is contained in one short and rather obscure paragraph but I think it illustrates the points I am making here. The argument is that maximin considerations underlie the choice not merely of the first part of the second principle of justice but of the two principles as a whole including the priority relations between them. He says that 'if we can maintain that the principles provide a workable theory of social justice, and that they are compatible with reasonable demands of efficiency, then this conception guarantees a satisfactory minimum. There may be, on reflection, little reason for trying to do better.' He adds that 'this line of thought is practically decisive if we can establish the priority of liberty, the lexical ordering of the two principles. For this priority implies that the persons in the original position have no desire to try for greater gains at the expense of the equal liberties. The minimum assured by the two principles in lexical order is not one that the parties wish to jeopardize for the sake of greater economic and social advantages.' (Page 156.) These quotations, which it must be remembered are supposed to be arguments for the rationality of choosing the two principles, have a circular look about them. The circularity is not quite complete (this must be so if they are not conclusive, as I shall suggest is the case) but the very strong dependence on special and extreme utility functions is evident. What Rawls is saying is that, if the preference-structures of the people in the original position are known by them to be such that they are not willing to trade-off any amount however tiny of liberty for any

6. The exception is of course that if the aggregate gains in wealth and power that can be obtained by pushing some a little below the threshold are so enormous that their summed utility exceeds that lost by those who fall below the threshold, the utilitarian solution is to choose that course. But in such extreme circumstances maximin would look less attractive—precisely because of this implication.

amount however great of wealth and power, provided they have some minimum amount of these, they will choose principles corresponding to these preference-structures.

My two lines of argument have been as follows. First, the most that Rawls could establish by this kind of postulate about the structure of preferences is that the parties would insist that if some specified minimum could be provided for all (the threshold amount above which increases are of little or no value to anyone) then it should be provided rather than let some fall below to enable others to rise above it. This 'minimum' is presumably to be conceived of in the light of Rawls's remarks as comprising the complete implementation of 'equal liberty' plus the achievement of a set minimum amount of wealth and power. But, as I have argued, the maximin criterion is not appropriate if the minimum achievable in a society applying the criterion *either* falls short of this set minimum *or* if it exceeds it. As we saw in Chapter 7, Rawls agrees that the priority relation should be waived at low levels of development but he nowhere concedes the further point we have been making that at a low level of development the maximin criterion for wealth and power may also be inappropriate.

Rawls does not concede at all that the principles are also inappropriate if the minimum achievable is above the threshold but as I have argued this is equally so. Here the priority relation between the first and second principles can be sustained but it is the maximin criterion for the distribution of wealth and power whose rationale collapses. As I noted earlier, one cannot get directly from aggregate to individual quantities. Therefore even if it is agreed that once 'equal liberty' is fully implemented and the societal minimum level of wealth achieved (which we might suppose to be defined as that which enables the worst-off to reach the threshold beyond which increments of wealth are of little or no value) nothing follows about the right distribution of income beyond that point from the idea that it is better for the society to be more rich than less. That it is better for the society to be richer than poorer simply reflects the fact that the remaining primary goods are already in maximum supply so there are no competing considerations. But provided nobody falls below the threshold there appears to be no case for saying, in the original position, that the society should be bound by the maximin distributional constraint once there is a possibility of getting everyone past the threshold.

The other line of criticism which I put forward is the broader one that if the people in the original position can know with complete confidence that their preference-structures have the form attributed to them by Rawls, then they can also be sure that the criterion of maximizing average utility will produce the appropriate part of the 'two principles' (that everyone should reach the threshold if possible rather than let some fall below to allow others to rise above it) while at the same time having the advantages of (a) providing more definite guidance than Rawls offers where the threshold cannot be reached at all and (b) not providing inappropriate guidance where the threshold can be exceeded. Lying behind this point is, of course, the more general one that unless Rawls's 'psychological generalizations' about preference-structures *are* true, the 'two principles' are definitely not the right thing to choose in the original position, whereas the principle of maximizing average utility does not depend for its attractiveness in the original position upon any special assumptions about preference-structures. And this is decisive if one believes that Rawls's psychological generalizations either are not true or at any rate are not so obviously true that it would be rational to base the choice of principles in the original position on their assumed truth. And it seems to me that it would be very hard work to avoid holding one of these two views.

Rawls's third 'special feature' of the original position was 'that the rejected alternatives have outcomes that one can hardly accept' (page 154). The most straightforward interpretation of this is that the outcomes of other choices may be extremely bad. This appears to be what Rawls has in mind when he explains how this feature can be found in the original position:

For example it has sometimes been held that under some conditions the utility principle (in either form) [i.e. maximizing either average or total utility] justifies, if not slavery or serfdom, at any rate serious infractions of liberty for the sake of greater social benefits. We need not consider here the truth of this claim, or the likelihood that the requisite conditions obtain. For the moment, this contention is only to illustrate the way in which conceptions of justice may allow for outcomes which the parties may not be able to accept. And having the ready alternative of the two principles of justice which secure a satisfactory minimum, it seems unwise, if not irrational, for them to take a chance that these outcomes are not realized. (Page 156.)

Assuming that Rawls means here, as his last sentence suggests, that it is unwise or irrational to forgo the certainty of a satisfactory minimum for the chance of a worse outcome (though a higher average expectation) the example is rather unfortunately phrased. For it leaves it unclear whether the case in prospect is one in which A's liberties are curtailed to provide additional social benefits for B (who already has a full set of liberties) or whether the case envisaged is one where A is happy to trade in a part of his liberties for higher social benefits than he would otherwise obtain. Rawls does wish to say that one point of the 'priority of liberty' is to prevent people from being able to make the trade even if they would wish to, but, as I have already observed, if the people in the original position knew that this was a desire that they might have they would not be rational to rule out the possibility of making the trade, or to put it the other way round, the rationality of choosing the priority relation presupposes that the case as stated could never arise. Let us therefore interpret Rawls in the first of the two ways I canvassed, as saying that the utilitarian principle might sanction making A worse off than he would be under the 'two principles' so as to make B better off than he would be under the 'two principles'.

What can be said of Rawls's argument understood in this way? I should like to list three objections, each of which has a rough parallel in the discussion of the other two 'special features'. First, Rawls's argument depends crucially on the idea that choosing a maximin solution (regarding the package of the two principles and the priority relations between them as constituting a maximin choice for this purpose) guarantees a 'satisfactory minimum'. We saw this same assumption explicitly stated in the passage quoted in relation to the 'second feature' and I pointed out that it is also required to get Rawls's argument in relation to the 'first feature' off the ground. All I can do here is repeat that this assumption is baseless. If the people in the original position are ignorant of all features of their society then they must of necessity be ignorant of the minimum position that would be achieved if a maximin criterion were to be applied to the design of social institutions, laws and public policies in it. They have no reason to suppose that the application of a maximin rule to their society will provide them with a 'satisfactory minimum'.

Nor is this merely a question of playing with the ignorance stipulation. If they knew that they were members of a contemporary society but didn't know which one, they could have no confidence at all that maximin would provide them with a 'satisfactory minimum'. If we take it that at the least a 'satisfactory minimum' requires having a diet with a nutritional mix suitable for maintaining efficiency and health, they would have to be aware that if they lived, for example, in India or many parts of Africa they would very likely fall short of this minimum. It may be replied that these societies are not organized on a maximin basis but, even leaving aside the questions about trade-offs between liberty and wealth mentioned in Chapter 7, it seems inconceivable that these societies could from their own resources provide everyone with enough of the right food to eat by mere reorganization.[7] Yet Rawls says: 'Since the parties have the alternative of the two principles of justice, they can in large part sidestep the uncertainties of the original position. They can guarantee the protection of their liberties and a reasonably satisfactory standard of life as the conditions of their society permit.' (Page 169.) The last clause in reality destroys the 'guarantee'.

Moreover, as I have also observed, it is highly implausible to suppose, as the people in the original position are supposed by Rawls to do, that there *is* a 'satisfactory minimum' defined as a collection of primary goods, the same for everyone, such that increases in the amount of primary goods have little or no value for anyone. Even if each person has a satiation point for wealth and power it is probably higher for most people than the minimum obtainable by maximin policies in even the richest societies.

Second, the plausibility of Rawls's example concerning the curtailment of liberty on utilitarian criteria depends upon the

7. Rawls does not say that there is any requirement of justice that rich societies should transfer resources to poor ones, even if those in the poor ones are starving. I take this up in Chapter 12.

falsity of his own 'psychological generalizations'. If liberty is more important to everybody than 'social benefits' (let's say material benefits) then just as it would never be A's wish to trade in his own liberty for increased material benefits to himself, so it would never be a way of increasing average utility within a whole society for the institutions, laws and policies to trade in A's liberty for increased material benefits to B. If Rawls is right about the structure of preferences, liberty must add more to the average level of utility than material benefits. The case as stated by Rawls therefore could not arise. We can make the point more generally without reference to Rawls's particular assumption about the 'priority of liberty' by repeating the point made earlier that if the utility produced by each unit of whatever is to be distributed is very high for each person up to some (identical) amount and thereafter very low, the attempt to maximize average utility will almost inevitably lead to providing everyone with that amount if it can be done rather than giving some less than this amount so that others can have more than it.

The third point is this. There is an exception to the assertion just made, as I observed when I first discussed the question. If the total amount of gain to others, measured in units of income etc., as a result of a small falling short of the threshold by a few people, were *sufficiently* vast, then even the fact that each unit of income that was lost reduced utility enormously more than each unit of income that was gained increased utility would not prevent the change from increasing average utility. But then the question is precisely whether, from the original position, it would be rational to wish to rule out the possibility of such a change's being called for by the agreed-on principles for the organization of society. Once again we seem to be right back at the question whether or not it is rational for self-interested people to maximize their minimum or their average expectations, and once again we find that when we have allowed for the way that the Rawlsian 'psychological generalizations' will, if true, modify the application of the latter criterion, we are no further ahead than we were to begin with. We appear to be forced back on attributing to the choosers an attitude to risk, and this move Rawls explicitly rejects.

But although Rawls does officially repudiate any use of

special assumptions about risk-aversion, he does in a rather vague way introduce them anyway in respect at least of the choice to be made in the original position by his repeated emphasis on the 'grave risks' involved, as if one could somehow establish the rationality of risk-aversion when the consequences of accepting a risk may be catastrophic without making any special assumptions about attitude to risk. This however is attempting to square the circle. A man with a neutral attitude to risk will rationally accept a small risk of a catastrophic outcome for a high probability of a moderate gain. It would appear that most of us are in fact willing to accept small risks of catastrophe: we take planes across the Atlantic instead of going by ship, we drive cars instead of taking trains and we travel instead of staying at home. As a society we balance off saving lives by spending money on road safety measures and medical services against other uses of the resources, and so on indefinitely. Since it is not *a priori* irrational to accept risks of catastrophe in this way it cannot be said to be *a priori* irrational for those in the 'original position' to be prepared to accept catastrophic outcomes. Nor can it be said to be rational: it really does depend on attitude to risk.

10

MAXIMIN AND SOCIAL THEORY

When one considers the earnestness of Rawls's endeavours to show that a maximin approach would be rational in the original position one can hardly fail to be struck by the relatively casual way in which he throws away the substance of the maximin criterion at two different points. One, which I have already mentioned, is in his proposed interpretation of the 'worst-off representative man' which would make him very far from worst off even in terms of primary goods. The other retreat is the one I shall discuss in this chapter. The point has some interest in its own right but is also essential for an understanding of the way in which Rawls conceives the commitment to principles such as his own 'two principles' or the rival principle of maximizing average utility.

Rawls states the obvious possible case against ever accepting a maximin criterion as follows:

The objection [that is likely to be made] is that since we are to maximize (subject to the usual constraints) the long-term prospects of the least advantaged, it seems that the justice of large increases or decreases in the expectation of the more advantaged may depend upon small changes in the prospects of those worst off. To illustrate: the most extreme disparities in wealth and income are allowed provided the expectations of the least fortunate are raised in the slightest degree. But at the same time similar inequalities favoring the more advantaged are forbidden when those in the worst position lose by the least amount. Yet it seems extraordinary that the justice of increasing the expectations of the better placed by a billion dollars, say, should turn on whether the prospects of the least favored increase or decrease by a penny. (Page 157.)

The answer that Rawls gives is that we know such cases cannot occur.

The possibilities which the objection envisages cannot arise in real cases . . . For as we raise the expectations of the more advantaged the situation of the worst off is continuously improved. Each such increase is in the latter's interest, up to a certain point anyway.

He goes on to say that

the difference [i.e. maximin] principle not only assumes the operation of other principles, but it presupposes as well a certain theory of social institutions. In particular . . . it relies on the idea that in a competitive economy (with or without private ownership) with an open class system excessive inequalities will not be the rule. (Both quotations page 158.)

What is so extraordinary about this passage is that in it Rawls accepts the relevance to the evaluation of social systems of the average (first part) and the spread (second part) as well as the minimum. All he is saying then in propounding the maximin criterion as a sole self-sufficient basis for evaluating the distribution of wealth and power is that if you make sufficiently extravagant empirical assumptions it will follow that what satisfies the maximin criterion will also satisfy other criteria. He recognizes that he might be accused of assigning 'Mr Herbert Spencer's *Social Statics*' the same status in relation to the original position as Mr. Justice Holmes accused the Supreme Court of giving it in relation to the constitution of the U.S.A. His reply is that

there is no objection to resting the choice of first principles upon the general facts of economics and psychology. As we have seen, the parties in the original position are assumed to know the general facts about human society. Since this knowledge enters into the premises of their deliberations, their choice of principles is relative to these facts. What is essential, of course, is that these premises be true and sufficiently general. (Page 158.)

Presumably acting on the maxim that attack is the best form of defence, he then proceeds, with remarkable audacity, to assail classical utilitarianism for requiring, in order to be tenable, factual assumptions which are not sufficiently certain.

I shall consider this attack later in the present chapter. Before this I want to examine Rawls's claim that the people in the original position would be entitled to base their choice of principles on a piece of certain knowledge: that 'up to a certain point anyway', raising the expectations of the better off must also raise the expectations of the worst-off. This agreeable notion that all good things hang together, so that a single criterion will act as surrogate for several (thus avoiding the necessity for messy 'pluralistic' trading-off of values) is most nakedly set out as the assumption of 'chain connection' (see pages 81–3). This might have been one of the happier inspirations of the good Dr. Pangloss himself. According to the doctrine of 'chain connection', anything which makes the worst-off person better off also at the same time can be counted on to make everyone else better off too. This, of course, instantly knocks the bottom out of most possible issues concerning the distribution of desirable but scarce resources of the kind which have given an edge to political dispute in the past few millenia. In satisfying the maximin criterion we can also satisfy the requirements of Pareto-optimality (that any change to be approved must make everyone better off, or at any rate some better off and none worse off) and although we may not quite maximize the average we can at least know for sure that whenever the worst-off is made better off than before the average is also increased. Moreover, although a society in which 'chain connection' held might not be one in which the distribution was a desirable one, the implication of 'chain connection' is that nothing much can be done about it: the poor can only be made richer if the rich are also made richer, and the rich can only be made poorer by impoverishing the poor further as well. The only room left for principles of distribution would be to choose between alternative policies both of which made everybody better off. (Thus on the maximin criterion one would prefer the policy that gave the largest attainable addition to the 'worst-off representative man'.) In other words, although redistribution, in the sense of making the well-off less well off so as to make the poorly-off better off, would be ruled out as impossible, there might be a choice between ways of distributing increments. Whether or not this degree of flexibility would be sufficient to leave much scope for purposive political action to produce a desired distribution of income cannot be deduced from 'chain connection' itself.

It would be easy to dismiss 'chain connection' as a bizarre flight of fancy, but to do so would be to miss the chance to learn something about the nature of liberalism and its presuppositions. For although the idea may never have been put forward so explicitly before, the only thing that makes it a curiosity is its being propounded in the 1970s rather than the 1870s. 'Chain connection' is a sort of living fossil, a coelacanth among ideas, alive and flourishing in Cambridge, Mass. If we turn our minds back to the nineteenth century we can surely see, for example, that the career of a middle-class radical like John Bright, from free trade agitation in the 1840s to the campaign for wider suffrage in the 1860s, makes sense only on the basis of a notion like 'chain connection'. It was indeed the stock in trade of writers of economic tracts addressed to the working class that any attempt to improve their position at the expense of others (by using the state's taxing and regulating powers or by trade union action) could only produce results from which they would in the long run lose. The most important single fact about European politics in this century is the general loss of faith in this doctrine, which on the one side results in support for interventionist working-class parties and on the other changes liberalism from a force which could see itself as 'progressive' to one which is either *immobiliste* or frankly reactionary. Classical liberalism is, one might say, a fragile doctrine, by which I mean that it makes a heavy draft on circumstances to be favourable. If hard choices have to be made it has no advice to give.

There are two questions to be answered at this point. The relatively easy one is whether 'chain connection' holds in all societies. The answer is no. Even if that is thought of as a too brusque dismissal one must surely at least say that it is too controversial to be treated as an axiom on which the choice of fundamental principles is to be based. The more subtle question is the general one arising out of this : is it ever sensible to hold ultimate principles which are understood to be contingent on the truth of various generalizations, even if they are rather better founded than 'chain connection' or the 'Aristotelian principle'? Rawls gains a Pyrrhic victory here, by taking as the alternative a ludicrously extreme one. 'Some philosophers', he says, 'have thought that ethical first principles should be independent of all contingent assumptions, that they should take for granted no truths except those of logic and others that follow from these by an analysis of concepts. Moral conceptions should hold for all possible worlds.' (Page 159.) No names are given, and I find it hard to think of anyone to whom it truly applies. In any case, starting this hare (or Hare?) does not dispose of the issue. What Rawls has to defend is the putting forward as an ultimate principle (not a mere rule of thumb) of a criterion of evaluation which he admits is not really ultimate, in that it is possible to conceive of situations in which an institution would satisfy the principle while being unacceptable because of its other distributive features.

Rawls says in effect, 'Yes, one can easily imagine situations in which the maximin criterion would be satisfied yet the outcome would be condemned because it was too inefficient or unequal; but since in fact such situations will not arise there is no need to worry.' Even if this were true, it would still seem to me a philosophically peculiar way of approaching the business of setting out ultimate criteria of evaluation. Would it not be better to start by trying to set out the real ultimate criteria and then introduce a rule of thumb for practical use? It would in any case be irrational for the parties in the 'original position' to agree to anything except the principles they really held. Rawls suggests, as we have seen, that the requirements of rationality in such a situation include a cautious, conservative attitude. They would surely not gratuitously assume the truth of Herbert Spencer's *Social Statics,* when they could instead agree to a mix of principles that made no such assumptions.

The remainder of section §26 consists of the attack on classical utilitarianism which I mentioned earlier in this chapter and also touched on in the last chapter. This throws light on Rawls's own position while, in my view, telling against it. He mentions the charge sometimes made that utilitarianism might be compatible under certain circumstances with support for slavery or serfdom, and comments:

To this the utilitarian replies that the nature of society is such that these calculations are normally against such denials of liberty. Utilitarians seek to account for the claims of liberty and equality by making certain standard assumptions, as I shall refer to them. Thus they suppose that persons have similar utility functions which satisfy the condition of diminishing marginal utility. It follows from these stipulations that, given a fixed amount of income say, the distribution should be equal, once we leave aside affects [*sic*] on future production. . . . There is nothing wrong with this procedure provided the assumptions are sound. (Page 159.)

This is interesting because it shows that Rawls thinks of utilitarianism as having, in the eyes of its adherents, the same status as the 'two principles of justice' have in his own eyes, that is to say as a principle put forward as an ultimate principle but which is really held only conditionally. Rawls's utilitarian, as presented here, would presumably feel obliged to abandon adherence to the utilitarian principle if he became persuaded that there was any likelihood of the facts falling out in such a way as to make grossly unfree or unequal institutions justifiable on utilitarian grounds. I should like to say that such a person is not a real utilitarian at all, but what one might call a fair-weather utilitarian. A real utilitarian, I suggest, is a tough egg who says that of course under normal circumstances maximizing utility does not lead to consequences inconsistent with our intuitions or sensibilities, but if you concoct a situation in which there would be a conflict all that shows is that you can concoct a situation in which our intuitions or sensibilities would lead us astray and need to be corrected by the results of utilitarian calculation.[1] He may, indeed, suggest the explanation that our intuitions, that is to say the maxims we have learned, are designed so as to be in accordance with the demands of utilitarianism in normal circumstances, but they naturally cannot be expected to have utilitarian results in bizarre circumstances—secret deathbed promises, six men in a lifeboat with no food or water, etc. In such cases our maxims give us the wrong answer though due to our training we may still feel otherwise.[2]

1. 'Whenever the conflict is a real one, . . . the genuine act-utilitarian will be prepared to jettison his "ordinary moral convictions" rather than the principle of act-utilitarianism.' Peter Singer, 'Is Act-Utilitarianism Self-Defeating?', *Philosophical Review*, lxxxi (1972), 94–104.
2. See the remarks on 'desert island' cases in P. H. Nowell-Smith, *Ethics* (Harmondsworth: Penguin, 1954), pp. 239–44. A recent real-life example of a 'desert island' case was that the survivors of a plane crash in the Andes

Rawls's only objection to what he takes to be the dependence of utilitarianism on assumptions about the way things hang together in the world is that it goes too far:

It is characteristic of utilitarianism that it leaves so much to arguments from general facts. The utilitarian tends to meet objections by holding that the laws of society and of human nature rule out the cases offensive to our considered judgments. Justice as fairness, by contrast, embeds the ideals of justice, as ordinarily understood, more directly into its first principles. This conception relies less on general facts in reaching a match with our judgments of justice. It insures this fit over a wider range of possible cases. (Page 160.)

But if 'justice as fairness' is superior to utilitarianism by buying at the cost of greater complexity a smaller dependence on special factual assumptions (a dubious assertion in my view) would it not be even better to go the whole hog and profess our actual ultimate criteria of evaluation explicitly?

If we try to do this my view is that it is useless to expect any simple principle (or even a set of them) concerned with *overall* distribution to give rise to the kinds of distributive judgements that we want to make in particular cases. Distributive justice requires a whole mass of different measures and the overall effect of this will be—what it is. For an illustration, let us turn again to questions of social welfare. If we believe that the objective of social policy should be, among other things, to iron out as far as possible the costs of sickness both in treatment and loss of income, an appropriate policy will require that those who are sick are made as well off as those who are like them in respect of normal income but not sick. Such a policy of redistribution between the well and the sick, holding normal income constant, cannot be deduced from a maximin criterion, even if we drop the 'primary goods' aspect of Rawls's theory and think in terms of want-satisfaction, well-being or what have you. All that we could get from a maximin criterion so interpreted (and with a more effective definition of 'worst-off' than Rawls offers) would be a system in which free or cheap medicine and *ad hoc* subsistence payments were provided for those who were very poor, while everyone else was left to his

who ate the flesh of their dead fellow passengers to stay alive for ten weeks on an isolated mountainside (*Times*, Dec. 30, 1972, p. 6).

own devices until his savings had been exhausted and perhaps those of close relatives too. Such systems are of course common, but they do not in my view answer the requirements of humane and equitable social policy. In spite of the superficial egalitarianism of 'concentrating resources on those who need them most' such a policy would not be satisfying to those concerned with social equality, because they wish to get the distribution of earned income right (and of course get rid of unearned income) but then provide universal social services. This shows that egalitarianism as an actual belief is not to be identified simply as a belief about the desirable extent of deviation about the mean but is a much more complex distributive doctrine.

THE NATURE OF
THE DERIVATION: A CRITIQUE

In this chapter I intend to put forward a general argument against the form of Rawls's deduction of the two principles of justice. The argument has a wide application against a line of reasoning which is often found among liberal thinkers, though it is possible to be a liberal on grounds which do not depend on its validity.

The general form of Rawls's deduction is as follows. Certain things (primary goods) are things that any rational person would sooner have some of rather than none of and (presumably up to some eventual point of satiation) sooner have more of than less of. Therefore, the principles that would be chosen in the original position would be concerned with distributing in the right way the largest possible amount of these primary goods, because each person would wish to maximize his prospect of getting primary goods. (For the purpose of the present discussion Rawls's two principles can be lumped in with utilitarianism. It does not matter precisely what principles are agreed on.) The point which I wish to make here is that, even if it is accepted that primary goods are things each person would (other things being equal) sooner have more of than less of, it does not follow that it is rational to choose, in the original position, principles of general application for the distribution of as much as possible of these primary goods.

An example will be the easiest way of showing where the logical gap lies. All else remaining equal, a motor car is something that it would be rational for almost everyone to want rather than not to want. This does not of course mean that it is in fact rational for everyone to have one. But if a fairy god-mother were to offer to provide one free of charge and pay all running expenses, it would normally be rational to accept. The only exceptions I think would be those who, like Mr. Toad, were dangerous drivers and more likely to be drawn into the temptation of driving by having a car on the premises. For anyone else a car, however little used, would be something worth having if it were completely costless. Does it follow from this that it would be rational to wish that everyone had a car? From a self-interested angle the answer is clearly no. The ideal arrangement for each person individually would be that there should be enough cars to warrant tarred surfaces and a reason-able network of garages but no more, and that he should be one of the minority of car-owners. If we say that it is not open to someone to specify his own position like this, because he is in an 'original position' (as with Rawls) or must state 'univer-salizable principles' (as with Hare), we cannot, from the infor-mation so far given, say what it would be rational to wish for with respect to the ownership of cars.

One possibility, certainly, is that a rational man faced with a constrained choice of this kind might wish for universal car ownership so as to make sure that he would own a car himself. But it might alternatively be rational to want a scheme under which only, say, the old and disabled were permitted to own cars. Or it might be rational to say that, if one cannot specify that one will belong to a privileged minority of car-owners one would sooner have the private ownership of cars prohibited, or even propose that mechanically propelled vehicles should be banned from the road altogether.[1] Which of these policies is rational depends on the value attached to the advantages of using a car to the user compared to the disadvantages in noise, fumes and danger to others. The choice that has to be made is between the individual good of mobility and the collective good of peace and quiet, freedom from harassment by traffic and the elimination of a large-scale source of injury and death. To contrast these as individual goods and collective goods is simply to say that one enjoys the mobility privately but one can

---

1. See E. J. Mishan, *The Costs of Economic Growth* (London: Staples Press, 1967), pp. 98–9, for a proposal that parts of the country should be declared out of bounds to the internal combustion engine.

get the benefits from the absence of cars only in common with everyone else. Both are individual goods in the sense that they are desired, of course.

The fallacy which I am imputing to deductions like that of Rawls should be clear, and I shall not belabour it with further examples, though they could be drawn from any sphere of social life. An interesting point about it is that it is the inverse of the standard liberal fallacy, which I take to be the argument that if a collective good is genuinely beneficial to all there is no need to secure it by compulsion since all those benefited will have an incentive for contributing to the cost of providing it. Thus, on this argument, the closed shop is unjustifiable because those who believe trade union membership to be beneficial to workers have an adequate incentive for joining a union anyway, so compulsion must be only a way of getting in those who do not believe in the efficacy of unions. Or again, it is argued that if a public amenity (say a park) is really wanted people will pay for it voluntarily so there is no need to raise the money by taxation. The fallacy lies in the illicit move from 'Everyone would gain if everyone joined (contributed, etc.)', to 'Each person will gain if he joins (contributes, etc.)'. It is a fallacy because it usually pays to be a 'free rider' if you can do so without general repercussions. From the fact that it would be better for me if everyone (including me) joined the union or contributed to the cost of the park than for there to be no union or park it does not follow that it is in my interest to join or contribute. For whether the union is strong or weak, whether the park gets made or not, is unlikely to turn on my contribution. Since everyone is equally in a position to think the same way, it is rational to agree on a system of mutual coercion in such cases.[2]

Rawls's illicit move goes along the same track but in the opposite direction. The standard liberal fallacy says, in effect, that if something is a collective good it is *ipso facto* an individual good; the Rawlsian fallacy says in effect that if something is an individual good it is *ipso facto* a collective good. It is an illicit move to go from 'I would prefer more of X to less of X, all else remaining the same' to 'I should like society

2. See Mancur Olson, Jr., *The Logic of Collective Action* (Cambridge, Mass.: Harvard University Press, 1965).

to be arranged so that I get as much as possible of *X*'. As we might expect from the formal similarity of the two fallacies, the snag is a variant of the 'free rider' problem. My extra one car does not add to the noise, pollution, congestion and danger on the roads an amount that *for me* outweighs the advantage of having a car. The addition is indeed, as seen by any given person, quite infinitesimal so it will not counterbalance even a slight desire to have a car. But it does not follow from this that it is rational to wish that everyone had a car. As we have seen it would be consistent to wish that nobody had a car, if one is choosing states of society.

Applying the analysis to Rawls's primary goods, the least discussion is needed by the case of wealth, since the extension from the car example is so obvious. Wealth is something that, for any given level of total wealth in one's society, it can hardly hurt to have more of rather than less, since one is not obliged to spend it if one doesn't want to. (The exception, as in the car example, would be someone who would be likely to spend the money in a way that made him more miserable in the long run.) But it does not follow from the fact that everyone would like to win the pools that everyone would like everyone to win the pools. It is quite rational to say that if you could specify your position you'd like to be a rich man in a fairly poor society, but if you're not allowed to make exceptions for yourself you'd sooner be poor in a poor society than rich in a rich one. An affluent society is a particular kind of society with its own advantages and disadvantages; whether one believes the advantages outweigh the disadvantages is a matter of judgement. It is certainly not settled, or even materially advanced, by the observation that people would rather have more money than less. The question of the optimal level of national income turns on the balance struck between the satisfaction that the consumer derives from goods and the costs imposed by their production (in pollution and resource-depletion) and often by their consumption too (noise, rubbish, etc.)

It is interesting to notice that Rawls himself suggests that there should be limits set to the average *per capita* income, but he does not give the reasons I have mentioned. He says that 'beyond some point' wealth is 'more likely to be a positive hindrance [to the realization of justice], a meaningless distraction at least if not a temptation to indulgence and emptiness' (page 290). Here Rawls's underlying puritanism really gets the better of him. Having enunciated the 'Aristotelian principle' as an alleged description of men's actual priorities he now says in effect that, just in case this isn't so, the chance of their being 'tempted' by 'indulgence' (i.e. want-satisfaction) must be kept out of their way. This is a dangerous line of thought for Rawls to dabble in, for if it is conceded that the opportunities provided by wealth may be abused, the way lies open to an extension of the argument to the liberal freedoms whose defence is the core of Rawls's book. In any case, although Rawls's private views may take this form, a deliberate restriction on national income is inconsistent with the declaration that wealth is a primary good and also with the maximin criterion as applied to income —especially if anything like 'chain connection' holds.

The application of our argument to the other of the 'interests', power, is, I think, overwhelmingly effective. If by 'power' we mean the ability of one person to get others to do what he wants, then power is obviously something it is advantageous to have more of rather than less, all else remaining the same. (There is the usual *caveat* about self-control, of course.) But it certainly does not follow that it would be rational to want to live in a society in which everyone had a lot of power.

It is important to see that the average amount of power in a society can be high or low, just as can the average income. A society with a low average is one in which people are able to exercise little control over one another's actions. As between households the lowest average was probably reached on the various nineteenth-century 'frontiers'—the West, the veldt, the outback—where settlers were little impinged on by one another or any agency of government. At the other extreme, a society with a high average level of power would be one in which people exercised much control over one another's actions. The average may conceal a gross inequality, as in the blueprints of *1984* and Calvin's *Institutes* or their real-life counterparts, but there can be mutual control distributed equally too, as among religious sects such as the Plymouth Brethren, Puritan communities of the kind depicted in *The Scarlet Letter*, and some utopian communities.

Plainly, whether or not it would be rational to prefer to live in a community with a high or a low average amount of power in it cannot be deduced from the statement that, all else remaining the same, more power is preferable to less. The inadequacy of the Rawlsian kind of deduction is, indeed, brought home sharply by the fact that everyone wants power, so power is a primary good, but everyone wants to be free from control by others, so freedom (the antithesis of power) is a primary good. Nothing could show more clearly that the question of the optimum balance of control and freedom cannot be solved by such *a priori* deductions from individualistic premises. In *A Theory of Justice* the crunch comes when Rawls equates the maximization of power with 'political liberty'. This, he says, is maximized by the institution of 'bare majority rule', i.e. a system in which anything a simple majority wants becomes a binding collective decision. But this may be oppressive and tyrannical, so maybe there should be entrenched rights to protect individual liberty. Political liberty has to be somehow traded-off against personal liberty, Rawls tells us (page 299) but his theory gives us no help in doing it.

I suspect that I may meet more sales resistance in suggesting that the Rawlsian argument for the status of personal liberty as a primary good is invalid in exactly the same way as those concerning wealth and power. Perhaps I should repeat that there are alternative ways or arriving at the ethical importance of personal liberty. The essence of my argument is that in choosing principles to apply to a society one has to look at the implication of any given principle for the society, and ask whether one prefers to have a society in accord with this principle or some alternative. I am denying that the answer can be deduced from individual *ceteris paribus* preferences.

I shall grasp the nettle and take up the case which Rawls regards as the paradigm of equal liberty: freedom of religious worship (and non-worship). The Rawlsian deduction here is simple enough. The people in the original position know that they may have religious beliefs which they will want to profess publicly. Since nobody knows what the content of his religious beliefs (if any) is, nobody has any reason for proposing that a particular religion be established as the only legitimate one because whichever one is chosen may not be the one he turns out to believe in. The parties in the original position have the possibility of agreeing that a majority (or some other group distinguished in a non-particularistic way) should be empowered to establish a religion and enforce conformity, but this again, Rawls suggests, would be imprudent since the result might be to establish a religion other than one's own. It follows, there being no other possibilities open, that the people in the original position will wish to write in as a fundamental principle freedom of conscience, subject to the proviso that the plea of religious conviction shall not be regarded as exempting anyone from the consequences of harmful actions as defined by the criminal law.

It may be asked where is the parallel with wealth and power? The fallacy we found there lay in looking at the beneficiary of an 'interest' and disregarding the costs he was imposing on others. But what is the cost of another person's freedom of worship? If the people in the original position are to assert that the claims of liberty are to be given priority whatever the actual constellation of preferences may turn out to be they must be able to know in advance that the cost of freedom of worship will be acceptable. But are they entitled to do this?

Once again, we have to remember that the choice between kinds of society cannot be settled by individual *ceteris paribus* preferences. If there are going to be private cars it is rational to want one; if there is going to be freedom for every man to (as President Eisenhower said) worship the God of his choice, it is rational to want such freedom for oneself. But looking at matters from the original position, the question to be asked is whether you prefer a society with private cars, or private Gods, or whether you prefer one without. You have to weigh the individual good of mobility or freedom against the collective good of banishing private cars or private Gods. The collective good, which, we have to face it, has been highly valued in many societies, is the absence of diversity, the absence (as far as it can be achieved by social policy) of religious doubt that is engendered by a common worship. 'I mentioned my having heard an eminent physician, who was himself a Christian, argue in favour of universal toleration, and maintain, that no man could be hurt by another man's differing from him in opinion. JOHNSON. "Sir, you are to a certain degree hurt by knowing that even one man does not believe." [3] If anyone would like to have the 'harm' that might be feared from freedom of religious profession presented more forcefully, here is the Grand Inquisitor in full spate:

Freedom, a free mind and science will lead them into such a jungle and bring them face to face with such marvels and insoluble mysteries that some of them, the recalcitrant and the fierce, will destroy themselves, others, recalcitrant but weak, will come crawling to our feet and cry aloud: 'Yes you were right, you alone possessed his mystery—save us from ourselves.' . . . The most tormenting secrets of their conscience—everything they will bring to us, and we shall give them our decision for it all, and they will be glad to believe in our decision because it will relieve them of their great anxiety and of their present terrible torments of coming to a free decision themselves. [4]

I am not saying here that it *would* be rational for people in the 'original position' to accept the views of Dr Johnson and the Grand Inquisitor. All I am saying is that Rawls's deduction aimed at showing they would not is invalid. The choice to be made is a choice between different kinds of society, each with advantages and disadvantages, a liberal society and an orthodox society. And I must observe here that Rawls mis-states the case by saying that the person in the 'original position' could not rationally wish for a majority-imposed orthodoxy because, although he would more likely than not be in the majority, he would not take the risk of being in the minority. For to pose the question in this way takes it for granted that the person in the original position will turn out to live in a pluralistic society, so that that question is whether to *introduce* orthodoxy. But if the people in the original position are allowed access to a body of psychological generalizations they will presumably know about the effectiveness of socialization. They will know, as J. S. Mill said in *On Liberty* (without seeing that the point could go both ways) that the same causes which make a man a Churchman in London would have made him a Buddhist or a Confucian in Pekin. [5] A society in which there

3. Boswell, *Life of Johnson*, p. 1015.
4. F. Dostoyevsky, *The Brothers Karamazov* (Harmondsworth: Penguin, 1958), Vol. I, pp. 303 and 304.
5. I cannot resist another quote from Dr. Johnson, if only for the splendidly characteristic conversation-stopper at the end. 'One evening when a

is diversity of belief and no impediment to the propagation of diverse beliefs is likely to stay heterogeneous; one in which there is uniformity of belief backed up by control over the education system and ferocious penalties for disseminating heretical beliefs is likely to remain homogeneous. One could, therefore, in the original position, take the line that one would hope to be in an orthodox society and if one were one would wish to have it kept so, but if one were in a pluralistic society one would not think it worth the cost (which might be to oneself) entailed in making it orthodox. On the other hand, only one generation has to suffer to create orthodoxy (as the absence of Albigensians in France and Jews in Spain illustrates), so from the original position one might think it worth prescribing the general principle that orthodoxy should be introduced if it does not exist; for the *a priori* probability of being in the minority (and a strongly convinced member of it) in a generation undergoing homogenization would be quite low. This calculation does not seem to offend against Rawls's strictures on probabilistic reasoning in the original position, since the only thing it depends on is there being a large number of generations, any one of which one may belong to. Rawls might, of course, employ one of his other pro-maximin arguments and suggest that it would be irrational to take the risk of very bad consequences (being persecuted for one's beliefs) even if the probability is low. But even if this general argument is accepted (and I have queried its cogency) it does not settle the present issue unless the person in the original position can be sure that being persecuted is a worse thing than can happen as a result of living in a non-orthodox society.

Everything thus turns on how important one thinks orthodoxy is. If it is as important as Dostoyevsky suggests, it surely

young gentleman [Boswell] tiezed him with an account of the infidelity of his servant, who, he said, would not believe the scriptures, because he could not read them in the original tongues, and be sure that they were not invented. "Why, foolish fellow (said Johnson,) has he any better authority for almost every thing that he believes?". BOSWELL. "Then the vulgar, Sir, can never know they are right, but must submit themselves to the learned." JOHNSON. "To be sure, Sir. The vulgar are the children of the State, and must be taught like children." BOSWELL. "Then, Sir, a poor Turk must be a Mahometan, just as a poor Englishman must be a Christian?" JOHNSON. "Why, yes, Sir; and what then? This now is such stuff as I used to talk to my mother, when I first began to think myself a clever fellow; and she ought to have whipt me for it." ' (Boswell, *Life of Johnson*, pp. 360–1.)

might be worth a chance of being in a minority requiring forcible conversion or elimination. After all, if the Roman Catholic Church had managed to suppress the speculations of Galileo and his successors, there would have been no Rutherford and no Oppenheimer—and even the biggest *auto da fé* never burned as many people alive as the bombs dropped on Hiroshima and Nagasaki did in a few seconds. I am not making the case, merely trying to show that it cannot be dismissed as absurd, which I suspect will be the normal reaction of those reading this book. Of course, even in an orthodox society a person in the original position will appreciate that he may be unfortunate enough to acquire a heretical belief which he will be prepared to go to the stake for rather than recant. This is an inherent risk, and again the rationality of running it depends on the importance attached to the benefits of orthodoxy. In a similar way, someone who chooses to have a society in which there is nothing faster on the roads than horse-drawn carts has to accept the risk that the lack of a fast ambulance may cost him his life if he suffers a serious heart attack suddenly. It is simply a matter of weighing advantages against disadvantages. The same applies to the extension from religious freedom to freedom of thought generally; indeed it is difficult to separate the two. I shall therefore follow Rawls in assuming that a separate discussion is not required.

It is not part of my brief, strictly speaking, to carry this discussion any further. But before closing the chapter I should like to follow up briefly my claim that liberalism can be defended without making use of the invalid argument analysed above. The way which sticks closest to Rawls is to say that when rational men compare a libertarian society as a whole with one in which only a single opinion is allowed they will prefer the first, because the desire for freedom is a matter of fact a stronger one than the desire to live in a closed society. Similarly, if we extend the question from freedom of belief to freedom of action, it may be argued that the desire to act freely is stronger than the desire to control the actions of others, except where these actions cause bodily harm or material injury. Thus we have a want-regarding reason for condemning any limits on freedom of speech, worship and action except that which is 'injurious' in the narrow sense given to the term by liberals. The snag with the argument is, of course, that it depends on the truth of a generalization about the relative strength of different motives which there is every reason to believe to be false. The desire to suppress views which are thought blasphemous, indecent or wicked is, it is perfectly obvious, a strong one with many people, and so is the wish to prohibit and (if the prohibition fails) punish behaviour which is thought wrong, even though it does no harm on the liberal definition of 'injury'. People who want to hang practicing homosexuals, horsewhip those whose personal appearance or clothes offend them, stop others from enjoying themselves on Sundays, make divorce difficult or impossible and prohibit the sale of cannabis, alcohol or contraceptives, may be considered unenlightened but the strength of their feeling is all too much a fact.

My own view is therefore that a liberal must take his stand on the proposition that some ways of life, some types of character, are more admirable than others, whatever may be the majority opinion in any society. He must hold that societies ought to be organized in such a way as to produce the largest possible proportion of people with an admirable type of character and the best possible chance to act in accordance with it, whether or not this satisfies more wants than would be satisfied in any alternative kind of society. Obviously, there are practical difficulties, and even second-order moral ones involved here, especially where (as in my view will always be the case) convinced liberals are a minority. One may recall here Roy Jenkins's argument against a referendum on British entry into the E.E.C. on the grounds that, had the institution of the referendum been part of British political practice during the period of the 1964-70 Labour government none of its liberal legislation would have passed. In some societies the minority of liberals may be so small and the passions of non-liberals so strong that a liberal society cannot endure. As Azaña, the Prime Minister and then President of the Spanish Republic said on the eve of the civil war: 'The only Spaniard who is always right is Azaña. If all Spaniards were *Azañistas* all would be well.'[6] But none of this affects the central point which is that, whatever a liberal

6. Hugh Thomas, *The Spanish Civil War* (Harmondsworth: Penguin, 1965), p. 145.

may believe should be done in any given situation, he must hold that a certain type of man, and a society in which that type of man flourishes are superior to others. Liberalism rests on a vision of life: a Faustian vision. It exalts self-expression, self-mastery and control over the environment, natural and social; the active pursuit of knowledge and the clash of ideas; the acceptance of personal responsibility for the decisions that shape one's life. For those who cannot take the freedom it provides alcohol, tranquillizers, wrestling on the television, astrology, psychoanalysis, and so on, endlessly, but it cannot by its nature provide certain kinds of psychological security. Like any creed it can be neither justified nor condemned in terms of anything beyond it. It is itself an answer to the unanswerable but irrepressible question: 'What is the meaning of life?'

12

INTERNATIONAL RELATIONS

I HAVE now concluded the main task that I set myself, which was to examine critically the central doctrines of *A Theory of Justice*. The book also contains, however, an extensive discussion of the particular economic and political institutions that Rawls believes would be compatible with the two principles of justice. A comprehensive critique of this part of the book would be an enormous task since all the most basic issues of economic and political theory are raised by Rawls's arguments in favour of a competitive economy and a system of representative government based on universal suffrage. There are certain points, though, at which a discussion of what Rawls says can throw further light on the central doctrines which are my main concern. In this chapter and the next three, then, I shall take up those points which in my judgement are relevant to the interpretation and derivation of the two principles of justice, and discuss them only from the aspects that are required by this aim. I shall organize the discussion in the three chapters so as to follow the order of logical priority within Rawls's system: the choice of an area within which the principles of justice are to operate, and the relations among these separate communities; the domestic political arrangements within each such area; and the economic system that, in Rawls's view, would emerge from the fundamental laws laid down in the constitutional convention plus subsequent ordinary legislation.

The odd thing about Rawls's treatment of the question how a particular community is to be defined for the purposes of the theory of justice is that he does not discuss it. Earlier contract theorists like Locke thought that it was necessary, before talking about the political arrangements that would be chosen in some sort of 'original position', to explain how the groups setting up independent centres of collective decision-making were themselves created. For this purpose they invented a preliminary 'contract of association' which (rather unpersuasively) offered a logical foundation for the rest of the theory. Rawls, by making it clear that as far as he is concerned the community already exists and its members have merely forgotten various things about its character and their place within it, may believe that he can dodge the question how the community is to be defined. But it seems to me that this is an arbitrary move which cannot be defended within the theory.

The idea, it will be recalled, is that the members of the community meet behind the 'veil of ignorance', which prevents them from knowing whether their society is in an early or late stage of economic development etc., and pick, as the principle to determine the distribution of power and wealth, the maximin criterion. But surely the first thing they would do would be to challenge the rules under which Rawls requires them to operate. Although they do not know whether their own society is rich or poor, they can presumably know that, if they live in the twentieth century, there will be a minority of rich societies and a majority in which there is undernourishment or malnutrition or, even if these are escaped, very little over and above the bare minimum of food, clothing and shelter necessary. Surely, then, the arguments which are said to lead the participants in the original position to insist on maximizing the wealth of the worst-off within any given community would even more strongly lead to an insistence that what this minimum is should not depend capriciously upon the good luck of being born into a rich society or the ill luck of being born into a poor one. The conclusion that existing states should not (as Rawls throughout assumes) be the units within which 'principles of justice' operate is not sensitive to the choice of principles. Whether we replace maximin with equality, maximizing the average level of well-being, or some 'pluralistic' cocktail of principles, we still get the answer that from the standpoint of the 'original position' the question of distribution between societies dwarfs into relative insignificance any question of distribution within societies. There is no conceivable internal redistribution of income that would make a noticeable improvement to the nutrition of the worst-fed in India or resourceless African states like Dahomey, Niger or Upper Volta. I do not belittle the importance, from a purely American or British point of view, of redistributing income internally. But the difference between one level of minimum income guarantee and another when both are measured in hundreds of pounds and thousands of dollars per head is put into perspective by the reflection that there are states with an *average* income of £14 per head, fifteen or twenty doctors per million population, and perhaps less than one in a thousand of the population in post-primary education.[1] Surely, viewing things from the 'original position' one would at all costs wish to avoid this kind of poverty if one turned out to live in a poor state even if this meant being less well off than otherwise if one turned out to live in North America or Western Europe.

Rawls does have a brief discussion of international relations, which he conceives in the spirit of a pure nineteenth-century liberal like Gladstone, not even making concessions to twentieth-century ideas to the extent of catching up with Woodrow Wilson, once described as 'Gladstone in a wing collar'. It is, indeed, significant that what discussion there is arises only as a subordinate part of a discussion of conscientious refusal to fight in an unjust war, and that there is no reference to the passage in the index either under the heading inter-national relations, law etc., or as a parallel entry to the lengthy one on 'justice between generations'. Rawls's conclusions on this topic are succinctly stated:

The basic principle of the law of nations is a principle of equality. Independent peoples organized as states have certain fundamental equal rights. This principle is analogous to the equal rights of citizens in a constitutional regime. One consequence of this equality of nations is the principle of self-determination, the rights of a people to settle its own affairs without the intervention of foreign powers. Another consequence is the right of self-defense against attack, including the right to form defensive alliances to protect this right. A further principle is that treaties are to be kept, provided they are consistent with the other principles governing the relations of

1. See the figures given for Dahomey, Niger and Upper Volta in Lloyd, *Africa in Social Change* (Harmondsworth: Penguin, 1967 (with revisions 1969)), pp. 331, 337 and 342. For nutritional standards see René Dumont and Bernard Rosier, *The Hungry Future* (London: André Deutsch, 1969).

states. Thus treaties for self-defense, suitably interpreted, would be binding, but agreements to cooperate in an unjustified attack are void *ab initio*. (Pages 378-9; the next paragraph defines limits on war aims and means of waging war.)

To derive these principles for relations between states, Rawls makes use of a device that he considered when grappling with the problem of justice between generations (the 'just savings rate'). There he suggested that we might 'imagine that the original position contains representatives from all actual generations' (page 291). Since it has already been postulated that nobody knows *which* generation he belongs to, 'the veil of ignorance would make it unnecessary to change the motivation assumption' and a 'just savings rate' could emerge (page 291). In fact, Rawls passes over this approach, for reasons which are not apparent to me since it seems most in line with the spirit of his theory.[2] But the point to notice here is that Rawls explains in the following way why the ordinary maximin criterion will not cover the problem of justice between generations: 'There is no way for later generations to improve the situation of the least fortunate first generation. The [maximin] principle is inapplicable and it would seem to imply, if anything, that there be no saving at all.'[3] (Page 291.)

Now these special difficulties do not arise in the case of relations between contemporaneous societies. A later generation cannot, by giving up resources, make an earlier one better off than it in fact was, but there is nothing to prevent rich countries from giving up resources to make their poor contemporaries better off. That the rich countries fail to devote even one per cent of their national incomes to aid, and that

2. He instead changes the motivational assumption so that the participants care about the welfare of their descendants. A little earlier in the same section, he discusses what appears to be yet another version, which would also be better than the one he finishes up with, according to which the parties again know that they are contemporaries (though they do not know in which generation) and they have to 'ask themselves how much they would be willing to save at each stage of advance on the assumption that all other generations are to save at the same rates' (page 287). Rawls's discussion is rather confused and he does not make it clear that this is a different idea from the other two.

3. This is because, if the first generation does not save and no later generation does, all are equally well off. But if the first generation saves this makes it worse off than it would otherwise have been, and subsequent generations better off. Therefore saving is contrary to the maximin criterion.

they refuse to co-operate in arrangements to pay the poor countries a high price for the foodstuffs and raw materials that they export is scandalously immoral but it is not the result of any logical or physical impossibility.[4] Even if the participants in the original position agree to play by the rules set out in *A Theory of Justice*, I do not think that Rawls's conclusions follow. He says:

Let us assume that . . . the persons in the original position have agreed to the principles of right as these apply to their own society and to themselves as members of it. Now at this point one may extend the interpretation of the original position and think of the parties as representatives of different nations who must choose together the fundamental principles to adjudicate conflicting claims among states. Following out the conception of the initial situation, I assume that . . . while they know that they represent different nations each living under the normal circumstances of human life, they know nothing about the particular circumstances of their own society . . . [They] are allowed only enough knowledge to make a rational choice to protect their interests but not so much that the more fortunate among them can take advantage of their special situation. This original position is fair between nations; it nullifies the contingencies and biases of historical fate. Justice between states is determined by the principles that would be chosen in the original position so interpreted. (Pages 377–8.)

I submit that the parties to an international convention under these conditions would not be satisfied with the principles which, we have seen, are put forward by Rawls. Even ignoring the question of economic inequality, it is remarkable that Rawls does not suggest that there would be agreement on any form of international organization like U.N.O., or a stronger version of it with a monopoly of weapons of mass-destruction. As far as economic relations are concerned, I can see no reason within Rawls's theory why the representatives of different

4. Is it necessary to add that the attitude of the rich countries is also, considered from the viewpoint of political prudence, about on the level of the French aristocracy when it refused to give up any of its privileges before the Revolution? Even if the poor countries are not strong enough to attack the rich, the turmoil into which they will be thrown as population pressure and poverty increase in the later decades of the century are, now that the nuclear super-powers seem to have reached a limited understanding with each other, the most likely cause of catastrophic conflict in the relatively short term.

countries should not, meeting under the conditions specified, agree on some sort of international maximin. One way of presenting the case for this conclusion would be to say: suppose that you were an embryo with a random chance of being any child conceived in the world in a certain period of twenty-four hours, what kind of world would you prefer? One, like the present one, which gives you about a fifty-fifty chance of being born in a country with widespread malnutrition and a high infant mortality rate and about a one-in-four chance of being born in a rich country, or a world in which the gap between the best and the worst prospects had been reduced? Surely, it would be rational to opt for the second kind of world; and this conclusion is reinforced if we accept Rawls's view that an element in rationality is playing safe when taking big decisions.

To sum up: first, Rawls does not and cannot defend the assumption that principles will be chosen in the original position by men as members of pre-existing societies rather than by men as men who may wish to form sovereign states or may wish to set up an overriding international state. Second, even on Rawls's own account of the way in which principles governing the relations between states would be chosen in the original position, his minimal liberal principles of non-interference and non-aggression are no more than a fraction of what would be agreed upon, if indeed they would not be superseded altogether by agreement on an effective system of collective security.

13

THE JUST CONSTITUTION (1)

ALTHOUGH I believe I have shown that the assumption is inconsistent with his own premises, I must, in order to carry through the discussion in this chapter and the next two, go back to accepting Rawls's basic idea that the choice of principles takes places among members of a single already-defined society. The 'just constitution' is a further development of this basic idea.

Thus I suppose that after the parties have adopted the principles of justice in the original position, they move to a constitutional convention. Here they are to decide upon the justice of political forms and choose a constitution: they are delegates, so to speak, to such a convention. Subject to the constraints of the principles of justice already chosen, they are to design a system for the constitutional powers of government and the basic rights of citizens. . . . Since the appropriate conception of justice has been agreed upon, the veil of ignorance is partly lifted. . . . [The delegates] now know the relevant general facts about their society, that is, its natural circumstances and resources, its level of economic advance and political culture, and so on. . . . Given their theoretical knowledge and the appropriate general facts about their society, they are to choose the most effective just constitution, the constitution that satisfies the principles of justice and is best calculated to lead to just and effective legislation. (Pages 196–7.)

This idea of a notional constitutional convention must of course be read in conjunction with what the 'principles of justice' are taken as having established as inviolate. When it is so read one might infer that the clause 'subject to the constraints of the principles of justice already chosen' leaves precious little to the convention except points of detail. For as well as the traditional liberties of conscience and worship, and the guarantee of the 'rule of law', Rawls also derives as part of the first principle of justice an equal right of political participation. 'The principle of equal liberty, when applied to the political procedure defined by the constitution, I shall refer to as the principle of (equal) participation. It requires that all citizens are to have an equal right to take part in, and to determine the outcome of, the constitutional process that establishes the laws with which they are to comply.' (Page 221.)

Now I do not want here to criticize Rawls's main conclusions about the 'just constitution', which seem to me, with their rather vague call for some appropriate balance between majority rule and entrenched individual rights, quite unexceptionable, especially since Rawls does not include among the entrenched individual rights the right to private property in the means of production, distribution and exchange. (In fact, as we shall see in the next chapter, Rawls believes that a socialist or a capitalist economy are both in principle compatible with the requirements of justice.) What I should like to do, however, it to draw attention to the nature of the premises upon which Rawls bases his deduction of universal suffrage, since this raises some general issues.

There are, broadly speaking, two kinds of reason for claiming that men should have a right to take part in the making of laws and other collective decisions, even if only indirectly by electing representatives. One is that each man pursues his own interests in politics and therefore any person (or at any rate any group of people with distinctive interests) who are excluded from power will be exploited by the rest. The other view is that politics is a matter of a discussion which is conducted from common premises, the premises being principles of evaluation —in Rawls's case the 'two principles of justice', since they are taken as the basic principles. On this view, the argument for universal participation runs as follows : each man has a potentially distinctive contribution to make to the discussion, which is improved by the presentation of alternative ideas about what is required to satisfy the commonly accepted principles, so the more people who participate the higher the quality of the discussion and, presumably, the better the resultant decision. This second view is recognizable in the writings of A. D. Lindsay and Ernest Barker, and is probably derived by them from J. S. Mill and T. H. Green. There can of course be intermediate positions. For what it is worth, my own view would be that those who share power are capable of carrying on arguments based on principles which have themselves as a group as their objects, but that if some groups with distinctive interests are excluded from power their interests are also likely to be excluded from the coverage of the principles used by the group with power.

The point of this discussion is that Rawls is a whole-hogger for the second view. He describes an 'ideal' legislative procedure, and defines a just piece of legislation as one that would, or might reasonably be supposed to, emerge from an 'ideal' procedure.

In the ideal procedure, the decision reached is not a compromise, a bargain struck between opposing parties trying to advance their ends. The legislative discussion must be conceived not as a contest between interests, but as an attempt to find the best policy as defined by the principles of justice. I suppose, then, as part of the theory of justice, that an impartial legislator's only desire is to make the correct decision in this regard, given the general facts known to him. . . . [This refers to the fact that 'ideal' legislation is assumed to take place behind a partial 'veil of ignorance'—B.B.] The outcome of the vote gives an estimate of what is most in line with the conception of justice. (Page 357.)

In itself the conception of a just law as the likely result of deliberation when all the parties are trying to be just is not, I take it, controversial. The most one might say against it is that it seems circular in that it is not much different from saying that a just law is a just law. What is controversial is the use Rawls makes of this conception in his discussion of the just constitution, i.e. the constitution that satisfies the two principles of justice and is in addition most likely to give rise to just legislation. For Rawls asserts that a just constitution is one which would produce just laws under conditions of *ideal* legislation.

The important point here is that the idealized procedure is part of the theory of justice. . . . The more definite our conception of this procedure as it might be realized under favorable conditions, the more firm the guidance that the four-stage sequence [principles, constitution, legislation, application to individual cases] gives to our reflections. For we then have a more precise idea of how laws and policies would be assessed in the light of general facts about society. Often we can make good intuitive sense of the question how deliberations at the legislative stage, when properly conducted, would turn out. (Page 359.)

That it is the ideal legislative process whose outcomes we are to use when judging constitutions is made quite explicit in the section on the 'four stage sequence' already quoted from.

This decision [the choice of a constitution] is made by running through the feasible just constitutions (given, say, by enumeration on the basis of social theory) looking for the one that in the existing circumstances will most probably result in effective and just social arrangements. Now at this point we come to the legislative stage . . . Proposed bills are judged from the position of a representative legislator who, as always, does not know the particulars about himself. Statutes must satisfy not only the principles of justice but whatever limits are laid down in the constitution. By moving back and forth between the stages of the constitutional convention and the legislature, the best constitution is found. (Page 198.)

It will be seen here that we are not to work out what fate proposed bills may actually expect, given the likely motives and tactics of citizens and politicians, but to ask how they would fare when put before an 'ideal' legislator, who did not know his special interests (or, I suppose, the special interests of his constituents). But as a basis for choosing a constitution this can make sense only if we take for granted that it is safe to use the legislative output under 'ideal' conditions as a guide to the reasonably foreseeable legislative output under real conditions.

Employing the terminology I invented earlier, this makes Rawls's constitutional engineering exceptionally fragile. He occasionally glances at the question what happens if it turns out that people do not behave in an 'ideal' way, and support legislation on the basis of self-interest rather than what they believe to be the requirements of justice. His answer is in effect that in such circumstances all is lost: not only can no just legislation emerge but the society cannot be prevented from tearing itself to pieces. If this is so, then the outlook is in my view a black one, for although political debate may be framed in terms of principles there are no societies in which parties and pressure groups do not pursue distinctive interests and in which their supporters do not choose them largely on the basis of a rough coincidence of interest.

Rawls contrasts politics and economics in extreme terms.

A peculiarity of the ideal market process, as distinct from the ideal political process conducted by rational and impartial legislators, is that the market achieves an efficient outcome even if everyone pursues his own advantage. Indeed the presumption is that this is how economic agents normally behave. . . . A just constitution must rely to some extent on citizens and legislators adopting a wider view and exercising good judgment in applying the principles of justice. There seems to be no way of allowing them to take a narrow or group-interested standpoint and then regulating the process so that it leads to a just outcome. So far at least there does not exist a theory of just constitutions as procedures leading to just legislation which corresponds to the theory of competitive markets as procedures resulting in efficiency. (Pages 359 and 360.)

This contrast seems to me very much overdrawn. In both economic and political activity people must behave within the general spirit of the institutions if those institutions are to survive. It is plain enough that representative government cannot subsist if a government defeated at the polls refuses to resign and annuls the election, for example. But free market competition depends on limits being set to the pursuit of money as parliamentary democracy does to the pursuit of power. I think it was Joan Robinson who observed that there is a certain incoherence at the heart of the theory of competitive markets in that it assumes the unconditional pursuit of profit by firms, yet the first thing rational profit-seekers will do is to collude, openly or tacitly, to control prices and outputs.

It is not, then, in question that some restraint in the pursuit of 'narrow or group-interested' ends is necessary for the satisfactory operation of a polity. But this leaves it entirely open whether it is sensible, as Rawls does, to conclude that we should work out the logic of the 'ideal' political system and simply say that any system in which behaviour departs more than a little from the 'ideal' is a write-off. The alternative is to ask whether a political system might still, with suitably designed institutions, produce fairly satisfactory results even if behaviour was considerably more self-interested (or group-interested) than 'ideal'. Rawls explicitly repudiates this approach. In the rest of the paragraph last quoted, he writes that what he has said 'would seem to imply that the application of economic theory to the actual constitutional process has grave limitations insofar as political conduct is affected by men's sense of justice, as it must be in any viable society, and just legislation is the primary social end (§76). Certainly economic theory does not fit the ideal procedure.' (Pages 360–361.) There is a footnote to the end of this passage, citing Schumpeter's *Capitalism, Socialism and Democracy* and Downs's *An Economic Theory of Democracy* 'for the economic theory of democracy'. The footnote continues: 'The pluralist account of democracy, insofar as the rivalry between interests is believed to regulate the political process, is open to similar objection,' and refers to Dahl.

I have myself written critically on both the economic theory of democracy and the pluralist metaphysic.[1] Nevertheless, this out-of-hand dismissal seems to me ill-judged. To some extent it is, I suspect, based on a misunderstanding of the scope of Downs's so-called (by him) 'economic theory of democracy'. Admittedly, Downs invites misunderstanding by the confused nature of his discussion of the 'utility' which is taken to underlie voting preferences. But it seems clear from his recurring statements of it that Downs intends 'utility' to cover anything that voters want out of the public policies adopted in their society. The 'economic theory' deduces the pattern and consequences of party competition for votes when the parties try to win elections and the voters choose their party preferences with an eye to bringing about the public policies they want—whatever the reasons why they want them. Now Rawls himself says that, even under 'ideal' circumstances, legislators would differ in their policy preferences because of, for example, different estimates about complex causal relationships. So we could put 'ideal' voters into a system of representative democracy and still use Downs's theory to say what would be the effects of party competition when the voters reached different views of the policies required by justice. Thus, for example, let us suppose that there is one major issue on which the voters disagree and on this issue

1. In, respectively, *Sociologists, Economists and Democracy* (London: Collier-Macmillan, 1970), Chs. 5–7; and *Political Argument* (London: Routledge and Kegan Paul, 1965), Chs. 14 and 15.

their preferences can be arranged along a continuum. The issue might be, among adherents of the 'two principles', the question of the level at which the 'minimum' should be set in the operation of the first part of the second principle.[2] Now, Downs's theory tells us that, in these circumstances, if there are two parties competing for the suffrage of the voters (and this is the kind of system Rawls seems to have in mind) that party will win the election (or at any rate gain most votes) which proposes a policy closer to that of the median voter than the other. In other words, the winning party will be the one proposing a minimum which as many voters think is too high as think it is too low. An implication of this, as Downs points out, is that both parties will have an incentive to approximate to the median position. I do not want here to enter into a discussion of the merits and demerits of this idea. My only reason for introducing it is to show that Rawls is mistaken in the final sentence I quoted ('Certainly, economic theory does not fit the ideal procedure') when 'economic theory' in this context is understood, as Rawls shows he understands it, to mean the kind of thing put forward by Downs.

This, however, is a bit off the main point. The essential question is whether, granted that *some* capacity to be moved by considerations of principle is necessary, institutions owing something to economic or pluralistic theory cannot take some of the strain off the motivational requirements. Can such theories give us grounds for believing that with imperfect human materials a fairly respectable legislative output may still be achievable? The answer might be put in this form: *given* the imperfection of the human materials, any respectable legislative outputs that do occur *must* be explicable in terms of economic or pluralist theories. Now Rawls himself apparently believes that a number of contemporary societies are 'nearly just', a 'nearly just' society being 'one that is well-ordered for the most part but in which some serious violations of justice nevertheless do occur' (page 363). He devotes several sections of the book to the question under what circumstances and for what

2. 'There is usually a wide range of conflicting yet rational opinion as to whether [the maximin] principle is satisfied. . . . A choice among these depends upon theoretical and speculative beliefs as well as upon a wealth of statistical and other information, all of this seasoned with shrewd judgment and plain hunch' (page 372).

purpose civil disobedience can be justified in 'nearly just' societies, and it seems clear from the the whole context that he believes 'nearly just' societies actually to exist, in the shape of the U.S.A. and similar types of society. I should be less happy to describe as 'nearly just' societies with such gross and pervasive inequalities of wealth and power. However, even if we go only as far as to agree that the social and economic policies of such societies are less bad than those of others, we are left with the question how this is to be accounted for. Is it that in these societies, unlike others, there is a pervasive overriding desire to pursue justice or (more generally) act on principle in political life? Or is it rather that the political institutions of these countries (and some other aspects affecting the distribution of power, such as the strength of autonomous working-class organization) give a more equal weight to the interests of all the members of the society than is found elsewhere?

Rawls plumps for the first answer. 'As always [in the discussion of civil disobedience], I assume that the society in question is one that is nearly just. . . . In such a society I assume that the principles of justice are for the most part publicly recognized as the fundamental terms of willing cooperation among free and equal persons.' (Page 382.) That the strength of the desire for justice is the distinctive feature seems to me highly dubious. Surely the impressive thing is the correlation between the existence of redistributive and 'welfare state' elements in public policy—even if fairly feeble ones—and a political system which gives the bulk of the population some share of political power; and the correlation between the absence of such policies and the existence of a regime such as those of Latin America (except Chile), U.S. puppet regimes in Taiwan, South Korea, Thailand and South Vietnam, and fascist or quasi-fascist regimes such as those of Spain, Portugal and Greece, that is to say regimes where power is concentrated in the hands of the 'haves'—usually landowners—and working-class or peasant organizations are suppressed. This does not entail that measures of redistribution and 'welfare' can be brought about only under democratic auspices. Non-responsible elites who wish to introduce them can, of course, do so. Communists have been the only examples so far, though in principle other 'modernizing elites' could do likewise. I should myself, however, agree with Rawls that the suppression of important liberties which is inseparable from elite domination makes these societies far from perfect; though, unlike Rawls, I am prepared to allow for the possibility of a politically repressive society with other advantages (perhaps Yugoslavia) being judged more highly than a society (perhaps Italy) which offers parliamentary democracy and, on the whole, the liberal freedoms, but is immensely corrupt and unjust in social and economic matters.

If we leave aside those regimes in which a self-imposed (or, as in Eastern Europe, externally-imposed) elite is committed to measures of redistribution and 'welfare', and compare those in which property owners rule unchecked with those in which power is more equally distributed, it seems to me implausible to argue that the significant variable in accounting for the different policies pursued lies in the purity of motives. Like most explanations in terms of 'culture' it invokes a cause which is too slow-changing and diffuse to explain the observed variations among phenomena, and in any case may be at least as much an effect as a cause.[3] Thus, if we find that the attitudes of businessmen and businessmen's governments are less overtly harsh towards the working class in democratic societies this may be because they cannot afford not to be, rather than due to some sort of Dickensian change of heart, just as the virtual slavery to which domestic servants were subjected by the English middle class in the nineteenth century came to an end not because of a moral revulsion against it, alas, but merely because domestic servants became more difficult to get as a result of changes in the economy.

It would be out of place here to enter into a detailed consideration of voting behaviour in democratic countries, and I shall simply assert that the evidence is consistent with a high degree of group-interest underlying party preference, though the strength of the correlation between class and party varies from country to country and is sometimes stronger in one class and sometimes another. To explain why democratic countries nevertheless produce more just legislation than those run by the owners of property is easy. The demands of members of the working class in different countries are fairly standard: a

3. See, for an elaboration of these general points, *Sociologists, Economists and Democracy*, Ch. 4.

reasonably paid and secure job with tolerable working conditions, adequate housing at a cost that can be afforded, sickness, injury and old age benefits and pension, free or cheap health and educational services. But these are also, I suggest, the primary requirements of distributive justice. It therefore can be expected that a society will tend to fulfil the requirements of distributive justice in proportion to the influence on legislation and public policy generally that the working class is able to exert.

Given his premises, the problem of constitutional design poses itself for Rawls as either very simple or insoluble: if people pursue justice single-mindedly it scarcely matters how the rules for decision-making are drawn up, since the results can hardly fail to be good; if they don't do this then all is lost. There is no room here for the conception of constitutional engineering that we find in, for example, Harrington's *Oceana*, *The Federalist* or Bentham's *Constitutional Code*, where it is assumed that the problem is to find a way in which the pursuit of self-interest can be channelled so as to produce good collective decisions. Bentham might have said of his proposed constitution what he said of his Panopticon, that its object was 'to grind rogues into honest men'. In both cases the means proposed were the same: a carefully constructed scheme of incentives and the maximum publicity to make the system as a whole self-policing. Indeed, it is difficult to see why, on Rawls's premises, there is any reason for the constitutional entrenchment of the personal liberties dealt with by the first principle of justice, since, if men behave justly, they will vote to preserve them anyway. Perhaps this explains why his remarks on the subject are so vague and tentative.

14

THE JUST CONSTITUTION (2)

WHAT, then, on Rawls's premises *is* left for constitutional design? The answer turns out to be a rather sinister one. It will be appreciated that the essence of Rawls's political thinking is that laws must be made by people who desire to do what justice requires for its own sake, and not because it happens to coincide with their own interests. Suppose then that we believe we are able to identify by their social position a set of people who are peculiarly well endowed with this desire. Will it not follow that these people should be given more say in the process of collective decision-making in relation to their numbers than the rest of the society? Admittedly, there is the little matter of the 'equal right to participation' guaranteed by the first principle of justice, but, Rawls explains, it is permissible to cut down one of the rights falling under the first principle to enhance the fulfilment of the rest; and, he says (citing Sir Isaiah Berlin) it may well be thought that the right of equal participation is less important than the other rights, indeed valuable only insofar as it is a means to the preservation of the other rights. (See pages 229-30.)

On the strength of these remarks he says that it would (given the appropriate factual conditions) be possible to defend as falling within the scope of the 'two principles' a scheme such as that talked of by John Stuart Mill in *Representative Government* whereby 'persons with greater intelligence and education should have extra votes in order that their opinions may have a greater influence'. On this view,

although all should indeed have the vote, those with a greater capacity for the management of the public interest should have a larger say. Their influence should be great enough to protect them from the class legislation of the uneducated, but not so large as to allow them to enact class legislation on their own behalf. Ideally, those with superior wisdom and judgment should act as a constant force on the side of justice and the common good, a force that, although always weak by itself, can often tip the scale in the right direction if the larger forces cancel out. Mill was persuaded that everyone would gain from this arrangement, including those whose votes count for less. Of course, as it stands, this argument does not go beyond the general conception of justice as fairness. Mill does not state explicitly that the gain to the uneducated is to be estimated in the first instance by the larger security of their other liberties, although his reasoning suggests that he thought this to be the case. In any event, if Mill's view is to satisfy the restrictions imposed by the priority of liberty, this is how the argument must go. (Pages 232-3.)

Rawls rounds off this amazing performance by bringing in the hoary (or should one say, barnacled) simile of the 'ship of state'.

The passengers of a ship are willing to let the captain steer the course, since they believe that he is more knowledgeable and wishes to arrive safely as much as they do. There is both an identity of interests and a noticeably greater skill and judgment in realizing it. Now the ship of state is in some ways analogous to a ship at sea; and to the extent that this is so, the political liberties are indeed subordinate to the other freedoms that, so to say, define the intrinsic good of the passengers. Admitting these assumptions, plural voting may be perfectly just. (Page 233.)

In the two and a half millenia since Socrates compared governing a community with exercising a professional skill[1] the fallacy should surely have been pointed out often enough. The passengers on a ship do not let the captain choose their destination for them. On the contrary, captains (or their employing companies) announce in advance where the ship will go and the prospective passengers choose a ship bound for where they want to go. Any captain (or company) persistently announcing unpopular destinations will go out of business. To the extent that this process

1. 'The people you will have to keep off, Socrates, are the cobblers and carpenters and smiths. They must be worn out now with all your talk about them.' (Xenophon, *Memoirs of Socrates* (Harmondsworth: Penguin, 1970), p. 41.) Although Critias' object of silencing Socrates was unlaudable I cannot help thinking he had a point here.

has a parallel in politics it would appear to be a system of political parties bidding for the favour of the electorate by offering attractive policies.[2]

Leaving this unfortunate analogy on one side, what is one to say of the argument attributed to Mill and Rawls's comments on it?[3] The idea that those with superior education will vote with greater disinterestedness than others is contrary to experience. The tendency is generally for the middle class to be more uniformly loyal to parties dedicated to middle-class interests than the working class is to parties dedicated to working-class interests. The one example I know of where extra weighting was given on the basis of a purely educational qualification is provided by the twelve British parliamentary constituencies made up of graduates, which with few exceptions returned rather undistinguished Tories.

In any case, it is not evident that a 'balance' is needed for justice, as Rawls assumes. I have argued that the furtherance of working-class interests is what justice requires, the second principle especially. The suspicion must be, I think, that Rawls fears the working class are less attached to the personal liberties of the first principle than would be implied by their lexicographic priority. This is the only meaning I am able to give to the idea that the members of the working class might be prepared to sacrifice equality at the ballot-box in order to make their other liberties more secure. For why otherwise should their renouncing power have this effect? If they were fully persuaded of the absolute priority of personal liberty they would presumably vote only for parties that were completely solid on that issue, whatever the rest of their programme might be.

2. Passengers on Oakeshott Lines are presumably uninterested in the destination since they sail a boundless ocean with neither port or harbour: see M. Oakeshott, 'Political Education' in *Rationalism in Politics* (London: Methuen, 1962), 111–36, p. 127. It may be recalled, however, that Donne (writing about a different subject) takes as the epitome of irrational behaviour going to sea but to make oneself sick.

3. I say 'attributed to Mill' because I doubt whether it is the main thrust of *Representative Government*. As I understand it, Mill is concerned lest, in the absence of proportional representation, a working-class majority in almost every constituency should result in working-class candidates sweeping the board. It was to avert this chimerical prospect that he proposed *either* proportional representation *or* a weighting for middle-class votes. In other words, the primary object was supposed to be to ensure a proportional middle-class representation under a winner-take-all voting system.

But this notion too has a paradoxical aspect when we reflect on the way the principles of justice are derived. For the priority of the first principle is itself deduced from the importance it would have in the eyes of those choosing principles in the original position. Surely there is something implausible in the idea that the argument for the priority of liberty would be accepted unanimously as valid in the original position but rejected by the bulk of an actual population? If those in the original position could be aware that, as members of the working class, they would be inclined to trade-off liberty for other goods, they would scarcely support giving absolute priority to it.

Rawls makes things even harder for himself by insisting that the working class should itself consent to the diminution of its political rights in order to safeguard its other 'liberal' rights. But how can we conceive of this as happening? It would mean their agreeing to be 'forced to be free'; but Rawls, with his 'thin theory of the good', is not in a position to talk about freedom as the victory of the real will over the slavery of appetite, etc. If the 'good' of the working class requires the reduction of personal liberty in order to secure some other end, then that's that: one could hardly expect consent to a proposal to increase the relative power of a class with different priorities. The same argument also applies to the notion that the working class might recognize the superior wisdom of their social betters and agree to give them more votes. To the extent they really believe in this superior wisdom they can be guided by it when deciding how to vote.[4] By this means they can refuse to follow the middle class lead whenever they see a clash between middle-class policy-preferences and their own interests.

We have seen how the 'ideal' conception of politics is consistent with the defence of disfranchising, wholly or partially, sections of the population. What of the alternative conception? If we start from the premise that members of social groups with distinctive interests will tend to act politically in a way that they believe to be conducive to advancing those interests, we may conclude that the more equality of power is approached the

4. This is how James Mill, in his *Essay on Government*, thought manhood suffrage would work out, in which he was much more nearly right than his son.

more nearly will equality of consideration for interests: 'No vote; no roads'.[5] This is not to say that simple majority rule can be expected in all circumstances to lead to just institutions: the coincidence of majority will and the requirements of justice is particularly at risk when there are separate and hostile groups divided by 'race', religion or some other basis of communal conflict. But we can, starting from such a premise, then ask in a realistic way what special constitutional provisions are required in particular cases—a question which, as we have seen, can have little point on the 'ideal' conception.

The assumption that the postulated operation of the 'ideal' legislative process approximates to the working of the real one has two more detailed implications for constitution-making which are worth glancing at before closing the chapter. The first concerns the so-called 'problem of intensity'. Some writers, especially Americans, have been exercised by the thought that under a system of simple majority rule a relatively apathetic majority may support legislation which is strongly opposed by a minority. They have held that if in such a case the policy supported by the majority is adopted the outcome is inequitable and also inefficient in the sense that the aggregate loss to the minority is greater than the aggregate gain to the majority.[6] Compressing drastically a large and complex body of literature, it can be said that three lines of political theory have developed among those who regard the avoidance of this contingency as a (perhaps *the*) key problem of constitutional engineering. One is to say that the system should be arranged so that the 'intense minority' *can* buy off the majority whenever their aggregate stake in the issue is really greater. Hence we get defences of 'log-rolling'—the practice whereby legislator *A* trades his vote on an issue he or his constituents do not feel strongly on in return for a promise of support by legislator *B* on an issue where

5. 'We knew the moment the Reserve [near Salisbury, Rhodesia] began because the road abruptly turned into a sandy, rutted track. As an African said to me: "No vote; no roads." ' (Doris Lessing, *Going Home* (Ballantine, 1968), p. 134.) At this time the territory was part of the Rhodesian Federation, but although its rulers were less uncouth than the present ones the general lines of policy were similar.

6. This is usually expressed by saying that the members of the minority could have compensated the members of the majority for the scrapping of the proposal and left both sides in a preferred position to the one obtaining after the measure has been passed.

THE JUST CONSTITUTION (2)

A is greatly concerned for the outcome and *B* not—and for the institutions (loosely disciplined parties especially) which make it possible. Another line, which is a variant on the first, is the 'pluralist' notion that it is a good thing if a political system makes legislative outcomes the result of a sort of parallelogram of forces in which the forces are represented by the exertions of pressure groups, because a pressure group greatly affected by an issue will put out much more exertion in relation to its numbers than one little affected. The outcome will therefore reflect numbers multiplied by intensity which is as it should be, assuming (as Dahl naively says in the *Preface to Democratic Theory*) that all interests have a potentially effective pressure group. The third line is an argument put forward by Downs in *An Economic Theory of Democracy* that the logic of party competition itself ensures that 'intense minorities' will get what they want because it will pay parties, in putting together their platforms, to court voters on issues where they feel strongly, for someone may vote for a party because he agrees with it on one issue he cares about a lot even if there are several other issues which he cares less about where he disagrees with it. This argument, however, requires that the intense minorities on different issues should be differently constituted, for if there is a single bloc who form an intense minority on all or most issues the party backing the majority view will get most votes, even if it is less intense.

Now Rawls will have none of these solutions. He says that 'in the ideal market process some weight is given to the relative intensity of desire'. But 'there is nothing corresponding to [the allocation of money] in the ideal legislative procedure'. Legislators are to vote for what they believe to be just, and 'no special weight is or should be given to opinions that are held with greater confidence, or to the votes of those who let it be known that their being in the minority will cause them great displeasure. . . . Of course, such a voting rule is conceivable, but there are no grounds for adopting it in the ideal procedure. Even among rational and impartial persons those with greater confidence in their opinion are not, it seems, more likely to be right. . . . The intensity of desire or the strength of conviction is irrelevant when questions of justice arise.' (Page 361.)

Rawls's insistence on arguing from the 'ideal' legislature to the most desirable constitution for an actual society blinds him, I suggest, to important distinctions here. In issues of general public morality—say the abolition of the death penalty—it seems quite correct to argue that intensity of preference for one side of the issue or the other should be considered irrelevant to the weight to be given to a view. In particular, I think it should be regarded as improper for a legislator to trade his vote on such an issue for support which would give his constituents particular material advantages. (Unhappily, this kind of corruption is common and it would appear an accepted part of the way a U.S. President goes about rounding up Congressional votes for his policies.) Further, it is reasonable to have a rule such as that in Britain and France (5th Republic) which prohibits anyone except the government from proposing legislation entailing more than incidental expenditure from public funds, thus avoiding 'pork-barrel' spending of the kind which is a noticeable feature of American federal politics. (This includes not just the traditional dams and harbours but, more important today, such things as the A.B.M. programme.)

However, there are many other issues where some group among the population are specially affected by a piece of proposed legislation or other public policy and where it is an advantage in a political system if there are ways in which they can exert an influence disproportionate to their numbers. On many matters there is no 'common good' in a strict sense, but a clash of interests and the issue is which interests should prevail. From the 'ideal' standpoint we are to assume that in such cases people will take up positions on the basis of their views about what is the just outcome, and no doubt feeling strongly about this would be no grounds for being given special weight in the decision-making process. But if we assume that in such cases people will tend to take up positions according to where their 'interest' lies (or more precisely where they perceive it as lying) there are good reasons for saying that the outcome is more likely to be just if those with a bigger stake in it have a bigger influence on it. The usual American discussions of the 'intense minority problem' are at fault in conflating the disappointment someone may feel in not getting his way and the anger he may feel at being beaten with the objective damage and disruption that may be caused to a group in the population by public policy; and the equivocation of the concept of 'intensity' itself reflects this. But Rawls, although from the 'ideal' stand-point he has no alternative, seems to me equally at fault in failing to distinguish between different kinds of issue.

The other question where Rawls's answer is determined (pre-judicially, I suggest) by 'ideal' premises is that of civil diso-bedience. The nub here is really the same as in the 'intense minority' question, except that we move to the stage after the 'intense minority' has gone down to democratic defeat and ask if it is morally legitimate for them to disobey the law in order to try to get the issue reopened. Take the case of a group of people who ask the County Council for a pedestrian crossing on a busy road much used by children, or petition the appropriate Minister to order a reduction in night flights from the local airport. If this gets no response would they be justified in, say, blocking the road at rush hour or sitting down on the airport runway? According to Rawls (who does not give examples— these are mine) civil disobedience is permissible when three conditions are fulfilled, and would be accepted *ex ante* on these terms in the 'original position'.

The second and third conditions are difficult to quarrel with, as stated by Rawls. The second says that legal means of redress should normally have been exhausted (page 373). The third says that, provided the society is 'nearly just', one should not engage in civil disobedience if the consequence of every-body else doing so on grounds no more strong would be the collapse of the society (pages 373-5). In itself this is unexcep-tionable, though there are two difficulties in applying it: first, Rawls has (as we have seen) no more than a few words about how to recognize a 'nearly just' society, and, second, it seems more likely that there is a continuum of stability/instability in a society rather than some single point of 'collapse', which again introduces trading-off problems—how much marginal instability for how much marginal illegal protest.

The first condition is that the legislation or administrative abuse protested against should be a clear violation of the first principle of justice or of the 'equal opportunity' half of the second principle. This would presumably rule out the cases I gave as examples, and (as Rawls explicitly says) all illegal pro-test based on violations of the maximin criterion for the distri-bution of wealth and power. The reason for this exclusion is, according to Rawls, that there is so much room for reasonable men to disagree about the implications of the criterion for public policy. It seems to me absurd to suggest that clear violations of the maximin criterion cannot occur, as in 1926, when the mine owners sought to reduce the pay of coal miners, and occasioned the General Strike, the other unions (correctly) reckoning that if this move were successful it would give the green light for wage-cutting in other industries.[7] The stipulation here surely stands or falls with the paramount importance of the first principle.

What, however, reflects the 'ideal' conception of politics, and makes the question relevant to the present chapter, is Rawls's discussion of the way in which civil disobedience may be carried out. The illegal act must be designed purely so as to draw the attention of the majority to the fact that there exists a minority whose members feel strongly enough about the issue to risk a fine or imprisonment. 'By engaging in civil disobedience one intends, then, to address the sense of justice of the majority and so serve fair notice that in one's sincere and considered opinion the conditions of free cooperation are being violated.' (Pages 382-3; for a similar statement see page 364.) This has two consequences for the definition of civil disobedience. First, it must be public and the participants must show that they are willing to accept the legal consequences of their conduct. 'This fidelity to law helps to establish to the majority that the act is indeed politically conscientious and sincere, and that it is intended to address the public's sense of justice.' (Pages 366–7.) And, second, 'while it may warn and admonish, it [civil disobedience] is not a threat' (page 366). It 'is clearly distinct from militant action and obstruction; it is far removed from organized forcible resistance' (page 367).

It is clear that these restrictions on the scope of civil disobedience follow Rawls's heaven-and-hell conception of political possibilities. Either a society is 'nearly just', and its members have sentiments to match, or it is a jungle, in which case militant action is all right (see pages 367–8). But if we adopt a more relaxed attitude, and are prepared to allow that a considerable

7. Whether or not the General Strike was illegal at the time can be disputed. By an Act of 1927, the relevant section of which has not been repealed, general strikes are now definitely illegal.

amount of human frailty may be compatible with a tolerable domestic polity, we need not commit ourselves to such sharp dividing-lines between methods of protest. Of course, in my example, the airport protesters have to permit themselves to be dragged away by the police, if the action is to be definable as civil disobedience; if they pull out machine guns and mow down the approaching police this makes the action a miniature civil war, that is to say a direct violent challenge to the writ of the civil authorities. But I can see no reason why the action should not (as in my examples) be intended to 'obstruct'—to hurt rather than simply to demonstrate in a special way. Once we accept the propriety of pressure-group activities at all, we should in all honesty go on to recognize that the usual legal means of exerting pressure on a government—threatening to withhold information or co-operation that the government needs—are of use to business and professional groups far more than to others. Political strikes and riots involving the destruction of property are the equivalents open to the poor. It is not that they are more effective (as is shown by the remarkable success of business and professional groups in all democratic polities) but that they are the only things available.

The essence of Rawls's high-minded conception of civil disobedience is the slogan 'This hurts me more than it hurts you'. The protesters are to break the law, but do it with such delicate consideration for others that nobody is inconvenienced. Why, then, bother to break the law at all? As far as I can see from Rawls's account, any public form of self-injury would do as well to make it known that one believed strongly in the injustice of a certain law: public self-immolation or, if that seemed too extreme, making a bonfire of one's best clothes would be as good as law breaking. Civil disobedience à la Rawls is reminiscent of the horrible little girl in the 'Just William' stories whose all-purpose threat was 'If you don't do it I'll scream and scream until I make myself sick'.

¹5

ECONOMICS

As we saw in Chapter 13, Rawls is unusual in maintaining dia-
metrically opposed psychological assumptions for the analysis
of politics and economics. Usually, those who deal with both
subjects are less schizophrenic: those who think the economic
system must be designed so that self-interest will turn the wheels
tend to think that political systems should be designed on the
same basis; while those who see politics as a matter of co-
operation for the common good are likely to think that economic institutions too could rely on men working for the common good. In favour of a single psychology is that economics
and politics are separated only artificially for the purposes of
analysis, but there is in my view much to be said for the boring
middle-of-the-road line that the truth lies between these two
alternative premises.

Let us see what Rawls makes out of his psychological premises. The first point to notice is that Rawls maintains the
consistency of the 'two principles' with either a privately owned
or publicly owned economy. The argument for holding that
the position of the worst-off members of society could not be
improved by diverting to them the interest and dividends paid
to owners of capital is not made explicitly by Rawls. (He seems
to think, indeed, that the tricky question is rather whether the
'two principles' would be consistent with a socialist economy.)
But the argument would, I suppose, have to take the form that
a privately owned economy is more productive than a publicly
owned one, and by suitable measures of taxation the worst-off
can be made better off out of the greater production than they
could be in a socialist economy. Since the question does not
affect the rest of the analysis and Rawls leaves it open I shall

follow suit, and concentrate on the distribution of earned income, by which I mean pre-tax income arising from a job. Much of what Rawls has to say on this topic seems to me admirable. I like particularly most of Section §48 on 'Legitimate Expectations and Moral Desert' in which he despatches elegantly the idea that pay differentials can or should reflect differences in moral worth between people. Having so often quoted to attack let me for once quote to commend. How neatly and cleanly the job is done!

The notion of distribution according to virtue fails to distinguish between moral desert and legitimate expectations. Thus it is true that as persons and groups take part in just arrangements, they acquire claims on one another defined by the publicly recognized rules. Having done various things encouraged by the existing arrangements, they now have certain rights, and just distributive shares honor these claims. A just scheme, then, answers to what men are entitled to; it satisfies their legitimate expectations as founded upon social institutions. But what they are entitled to is not proportional to nor dependent upon their intrinsic worth. The principles of justice that regulate the basic structure and specify the duties and obligations of individuals do not mention moral desert, and there is no tendency for distributive shares to correspond to it. (Page 311.)

'Thus', he sums up crunchingly,

the concept of moral worth is secondary to those of right and justice, and it plays no role in the substantive definition of distributive shares. The case is analogous to the relation between the substantive rules of property and the law of robbery and theft. These offenses and the demerits they entail presuppose the institution of property which is established for prior and independent social ends. For a society to organize itself with the aim of rewarding moral desert as a first principle would be like having the institution of property in order to punish thieves. (Page 313.)[1]

This implies, as Rawls makes clear, that no considerations of desert or moral worth underlie differentials in earned income.

Surely a person's moral worth does not vary according to how many offer similar skills or happen to want what he can produce. No one supposes that when someone's abilities are less in demand or have

1. For a specimen of the view Rawls is attacking here see W. G. Runciman's *Relative Deprivation and Social Justice*, Part 4.

deteriorated (as in the case of singers) his moral deservingness undergoes a similar shift. . . . It is one of the fixed points of our moral judgements that no one deserves his place in the distribution of natural assets any more than he deserves his initial starting place in society. (Page 311.)

The part that I wish to query comes after this one. Given these moral premises one might normally expect egalitarian conclusions about the justifiable spread of differentials to follow. That they do not is due to Rawls's insistence that people must be paid their marginal product in order to attract them into the occupations where they are most needed and once there induce them to perform conscientiously. Because of the importance of incentives he believes that differentials should not be whittled away by progressive taxation but that direct taxes should be levied at a rate that makes them proportional to income or, perhaps better, expenditure. (See pages 278-9.) Underlying this is the belief that once we assume self-interested behaviour we must be prepared for large differentials in post-tax income.

Rawls is not very clear about the precise form taken by his psychological assumptions, and the safest thing is, I think, to try to infer them from his description of the differentials that he believes would be necessary under conditions of 'fair equality of opportunity': 'The premiums earned by scarce natural talents, for example, are to cover the costs of training and to encourage the efforts of learning, as well as to direct ability to where it best furthers the common interest.' (Page 311.) If we look at Rawls's explicit statements about his psychological premises we find, I suggest, that they blur the crucial issues. He says, in defence of a competitive market economy (whether publicly or privately owned) that 'the theory of justice assumes a definite limit on the strength of social and altruistic motivation. It supposes that individuals and groups put forward competing claims, and while they are willing to act justly, they are not prepared to abandon their interests. There is no need to elaborate further that this presumption does not imply that men are selfish in the ordinary sense.' (Page 281.) We can see how little this gets to grips with the central issue if we reflect that it is a statement that could be made equally about Rawlsian politics and Rawlsian economics. Where's the catch, then?

Surely the catch lies in the fact that everything turns on what in any given case is taken as constituting 'abandoning one's interests' and on how much of a constraint on the pursuit of self-interest is imposed by a 'willingness to act justly'.

In politics, a willingness to act justly is a severe constraint: it requires, according to Rawls, that people should pursue not their own interests but whatever outcome they believe to be on the whole the most just. But in economic life the constraints imposed by Rawls are minimal, so that self-interested behaviour will usually also count as just behaviour in that it is not contrary to the requirements of justice. It is misleading in this case to say that people are not assumed to be selfish in the ordinary sense, because the proviso that they are willing to accept the requirements of justice sets no significant limits on the pursuit of self-interest. As Rawls puts it, begging all the questions: 'Assuming that everyone accepts the priority of self- or group-interested motivation duly regulated by a sense of justice, each decides to do those things that best accord with his aims. Variations in wages and income and the perquisites of position are simply to influence these choices so that the end result accords with efficiency and justice.' (Page 315.)

I should like to put forward two possible psychological assumptions which would both suggest the possibility of a more egalitarian distribution of earned income than Rawls allows for. The first is a minimal departure from the most extreme self-interest, and would seem to be within the spirit of Rawls's general remarks quoted above, though it seems clear that he does not make it in the case of economics. This assumption is that people are capable of eschewing self-interest to the extent of not being dogs in mangers. By a dog in a manger I mean (going beyond the usual meaning) someone who would prefer to do X on certain terms to not doing X, if those were definitely the only alternatives, but who refuses to agree to do it because it will bestow a net benefit on someone else which he hopes to divert to himself in the form of improved terms. This is best explained by an example. Suppose (to take an extreme but not impossible one) there exists a pop singer who, if the choice were narrowed down to the two alternatives, would sooner make six records a year for £1000 than work as a bus conductor (his other available choice), while the record company could pay him a royalty of £100,000 a year and still make a standard profit on the deal. There are £99,000 of surplus, or economic rent, to be bargained for between the singer and the company. In a profit-oriented economy it would be only reasonable to expect the singer to stick out for all or nearly all of the £100,000. The record company will charge whatever is the most profitable price for the records anyway so the only result of settling for less is to put more money in the shareholders' pockets. The non-dog-in-manger assumption does not require such quixotic behaviour, which in any case would make the distribution of income even more inequitable by increasing the share of unearned income. What it does say is that it would be possible to have a society in which, on the understanding that others were doing likewise and that the economic rent forgone would not be a source of private profit, people would be willing to work for pay which made their occupation attractive on balance without behaving as dogs in mangers.

The proposition here is that such a society could be stable in the same sense as that in which Rawls asserts a just society (on his specification of justice) could be stable, that is to say that there exist in human nature potentially adequate motivating forces to enable a society so organized to maintain itself as a going concern without needing recourse to a massive level of coercion. 'A massive level of coercion' means, roughly speaking, coercion that has to be applied so as to achieve compliance with the rules, as against coercion which is necessary (as far as the great majority are concerned) only to guarantee that their own compliance is not taken advantage of by 'free riders'.[2] As does Rawls, I assume that the normal methods of socialization would be in line with the required motivation: that schools would encourage collaboration rather than competition among their pupils, for example. And, again following Rawls, I assume that the other institutions of society would be made compatible with it. Thus, if differential social status were awarded

2. This second kind of coercion is an unavoidable necessity where the 'free rider' problem exists. Hobbes, who is often understood as arguing for the necessity of coercion to get people to obey the sovereign, in my view argues rather for the second kind, and indeed says that no stable society could be founded upon the first. See my 'Warrender and his Critics' reprinted in R. S. Peters (ed.), *Hobbes and Rousseau* (New York: Doubleday, 1972), 37–65.

at all, it would be necessary for it to be clearly on the basis of performing a valuable public service and not mediated by money. The argument of doctors and other professionals that they have to be paid a lot or they will not be respected sufficiently would therefore be undercut at its source. (This is leaving aside the question whether, even in existing societies, those professionals who do supply a public service—and not all do—would not be adequately respected whatever they were paid.)

How important the non-dog-in-manger assumption is for the degree of equality achievable in earned income depends, of course, on how much economic rent goes to the higher-paid earners in contemporary societies. My own guess is that enough people with professional and managerial jobs really like them (and enough others who would enjoy them and have sufficient ability to do them are waiting to replace those who do not) to enable the pay of these jobs to be brought down considerably, if people were to take jobs which provided a net benefit to themselves without worrying about how much more they could extract by sticking up the community. To put a rough figure on it, I would suggest that the pay levels in Britain of school-teachers and social workers seem to offer net rewards which recruit and maintain just enough people, and that this provides a guideline to the pay levels that could be sustained generally among professionals and managers, allowing a certain amount extra for jobs without security of tenure and especially arduous conditions.

In support of this one might bear in mind Rawls's 'Aristotelian principle'. I admit to having had some fun with this earlier, and would still maintain that the idea of most people wanting to spend all their lives at full stretch seems implausible. But that does not mean that there is not a desire—common enough to be important though far from universal—to spend at any rate a part of one's life in a way which challenges and extends one's abilities. And there is a wealth of evidence that for many people this experience is best found in their paid occupation. We could not otherwise explain why a man works at a job requiring the exercise of skill when he could get better pay as an unskilled or semiskilled worker on an assembly line, or why a man will throw up a well-paid and relatively undemanding job in mid-career to take up the arduous and financially uncertain life of a writer or artist. The threats of doctors and managers to become dustmen unless their pay is high are, I suggest, more likely to express dog-in-the-manger sentiments than to reflect a genuine belief that, given a straight choice between their own job and that of a dustman at the same pay, with no chance of bargaining for other deals, they would prefer the life of a dustman. For a similiar reason I do not think it is necessary to accept Rawls's assumption that a sufficient supply of highly educated people will be forthcoming only if lured by the anticipation of a higher income afterwards as a result.[3]

None of this, of course, shows that it would be possible to have a society in which people forswore the attempt to extract the last penny the community would be prepared to pay rather than dispense with their services altogether, and settled for a level of pay that made their chosen occupation more attractive on balance than any alternative. No society has tried the experiment in favourable enough conditions to give useful guidance. Thus, the Eastern European countries introduced strongly egalitarian pay structures after the post-war Communist seizure of power, but since these measures were associated with inefficient and rigid economic planning, political repression and subservience to and exploitation by the Soviet Union, it is hardly to be wondered at that the whole package was extremely

3. It would also be rash to assume that it would be an economic loss if fewer sought higher education. The educational qualifications required for entrance to occupations are simply a reflection of the proportion of the age group receiving higher education. As the proportion increases employers find that they can raise the standards of educational qualification required for entry at each level, and indeed must do so if they are to recruit people with the same ability as before. This does not in any way prove that the higher qualifications actually make them better at the job. Now that banks recruit graduates everyone has his own personal banking atrocity story. When the only thing needed by bank clerks was the school certificate one gathers bank statements were usually correct and standing orders were neither unpaid nor paid twice. The trouble is that the situation is, from the standpoint of a given group of eighteen-years-olds, a prisoner's dilemma one. Collectively, they will finish up in whatever slots the economy provides, and there is no mechanism to adapt the composition of the work force according to the distribution of educational qualifications among new entrants into the economy; but individually, each can steal a march on the rest by getting a higher qualification. This rather cruel hoax played on the young, by which each successive cohort has to run faster to stay in the same place, can only be alleviated by removing the financial rewards of higher education so that those who seek it either want it for its own sake or at any rate want the jobs for which it is really required for their own sake.

unpopular. Sweden is probably the country in which the government and unions have gone furthest towards trying to level
incomes at source, as well as having progressive taxation, and
this has recently resulted in counter-attacks by the professionals,
even including strikes. But although the policy of equalization
has not had the same disadvantages as those in Eastern Europe,
it has suffered from one difficulty which may be crucial. In spite
of forty years of predominantly social democratic government,
Sweden still has a privately owned economy, and it may well
be that those with a title to high incomes in virtue of having
earned them will always resent having their advantage over the
average man whittled away so as to leave as the only wealthy
people those with unearned incomes. Even if this obstacle were
removed, it is still necessary to reckon with the obstinate conviction of people in middle-class occupations that they *ought*
to be paid more, and in particular perhaps the idea that, if *A*
regularly gives orders to *B*, *A* should be paid more than *B*.
This is easily enough explicable as a survival from the period
(covering most of the history of civilization) when those who
gave orders were indeed almost a different category of human
beings, with an entirely different style of life. The question is
whether this survival can gradually disappear. It has surely been
considerably attenuated in the last hundred years so there seems
no impossibility in it.

Detailed discussion of practical problems would be out of
place here, so I shall merely add two practical notes. First, it is
clear that what we are talking about here is an incomes policy
backed by legal sanctions and run as a permanent instrument
of social justice, not as a short-term expedient to impress
foreign bankers with the government's determination to 'bash
the unions'.[4] Second, in any discussion of the possibilities of
equalizing earned incomes it is always pointed out sooner or
later that this might lead certain categories of skilled professional to emigrate *en bloc* with disastrous consequences. This
would not, it should be observed, be dog-in-the-manger behaviour, because the opportunity to earn more is (we suppose)
actually open. It is therefore worth briefly looking at the problem. When it comes down to it, the only two groups whose

4. See on this Hugh Clegg, *How to Run an Incomes Policy and Why We
Made Such a Mess of the Last One* (London: Heinemann, 1971).

members look at all likely to defect on a large scale are airline pilots and doctors. (The idea, put about by British businessmen, that other countries are waiting to snap them up is merely funny.) There are three possible responses. One is to recognize a stick-up when one is faced with one, and make a hole in the incomes policy big enough to accommodate these two groups. Alternatively, still acting unilaterally, a country could decide to do without them. Airlines are not profitable, and it might be quite advantageous to be almost the only country in the world without one, and let Ethiopian Airlines, Air Zaire and the rest carry the losses, if they choose to. Doctors are less dispensable, but over time it would be possible to replace G.P.s with people having a lower (and less marketable) qualification, and keep the hole in the incomes policy down to a cadre of specialists. The third possibility is an international non-poaching agreement.

I have now explored the implications of the minimum de· parture from an extreme self-interest assumption, the non-dog· in-manger assumption. The larger departure would be of course to assume that in a society with suitable other institutions people would be willing to regard the fact that some job needed doing as itself a salient motive for doing it. If this were so then the need for pay differentials would be greatly reduced. This motive exists to some degree even in existing societies and would, it seems reasonable to expect, increase in power within a non-dog-in-manger society. But my own view for what it is worth is that it is asking too much to imagine that it would ever be possible in a large society simply to pay everyone the same and point out what jobs needed doing. It might be done within an anarcho-syndicalist framework where the largest economically independent unit was a hundred or so strong, but even this might well involve a good deal of brow-beating, which is a high price to pay for eliminating income differentials, and there are of course massive practical problems inherent in any such economic structure. In any case, the issue here is clear and does not, I think, need lengthy discussion, especially since (as I have suggested) whatever the ultimate possibilities the anti-dog-in-manger stage would have to come first.

So much for pay differentials. But there is another aspect of the occupational system which needs attention, namely the content of the jobs themselves. It is characteristic of Rawls's liberalism that for him the paramount value in relation to occupations is freedom of choice. We saw earlier how the principle of 'fair equality of opportunity' is given priority over the maximin criterion and derived from the higher-level primary goods. Even if markets do not work out according to the postulates of free market competition, this, says Rawls, is 'not especially worrisome. It is more important that a competitive scheme gives scope for the principle of free association and individual choice of occupation against a background of fair equality of opportunity . . . A basic prerequisite [of justice] is the compatibility of economic arrangements with the institutions of liberty and free association.' (Page 310.)

Certainly the importance for human happiness of a free choice of occupation is not to be scoffed at, but it is no panacea. There is a strong formal similarity between freedom of choice of occupation and the freedom of choice of schools offered by a selective system of secondary education. The parents of a child of, say, average intelligence who were naive enough to believe that 'freedom of choice' meant that they could choose a grammer school would soon learn better. This is a sort of looking-glass freedom—it only works in one direction. If their child had qualified to go to a grammer school, they would have had the freedom of choice of sending it to a secondary modern school instead! In exactly the same way it is open to a university graduate to be a dustman but it is not open to a fifteen-year-old school-leaver to become a professional. Just as rich and poor are free to sleep under the bridges of the Seine so graduates and fifteen-year-old school-leavers are free to be dustmen. The difference between the case of jobs and schools is that there do not need to be more and less attractive schools, and should not be; but the existence of more and less attractive jobs (and hence some method of selection) seems unavoidable.

The usual liberal response to this is to say, as Rawls does, that there's nothing to be done about the range of jobs available, and the important thing is a fair competition for the interesting and enjoyable ones. But Rawls is not entirely a standard liberal. Although he is, in his social theory, a lineal descendent of Herbert Spencer, he has in his moral theory the maximin criterion. However watered down and low-ranked it may be it still rules out letting the devil take the hindmost. Instead of playing up competition for the good jobs, it seems to me that, even within Rawls's own theory, it is a matter of justice to make the less attractive positions in the occupational system as good as possible.

Rawls addresses himself to this question in two places. In the first he says, 'What men want is meaningful work in free association with others . . .' and adds, in brackets, 'Of course, the definition of meaningful work is a problem in itself. Though it is not a problem of justice, a few remarks in Part Three are addressed to it.' (Page 290.) Unusually, no cross-reference is given, and there is also no relevant entry in the index. The only remarks I have been able to find in Part Three bearing on the topic are as follows: 'To be sure, the worst aspects of [the division of labour] can be surmounted: no one need be servilely dependent on others and made to choose between monotonous and routine occupations which are deadening to human thought and sensibility. Each can be offered a variety of tasks so that the different elements of his nature find suitable expression.' (Page 529.) It is noteworthy that Rawls does not consider the question of improving the working conditions of the bulk of the population as one of justice. This ties in with the casual treatment the subject gets—we might compare with this total of four sentences the whole section plus a number of pages elsewhere devoted to equality of opportunity—and also with the fact that Rawls suggests no machinery for bringing about the changes he so airily speaks of as being possible. One is forced to conclude that he must believe market forces to have some inherent tendency to bring them about, which is completely contradictory to experience.

Since Rawls does not suggest ways of improving things, let me mention two, and let me say also that the question is not merely one of monotonous or routine jobs but jobs that are filthy, exhausting and injurious to health. The first line of attack would be to spread the nastiest jobs around by requiring everyone, before entering higher education or entering a profession, to do, say, three years of work wherever he or she was directed. (This would also have educational advantages.) To supplement this there could be a call-up of say a month every year, as with the Swiss and Israeli armed forces but directed towards peaceful occupations. These steps would of course constitute a limited interference of occupational choice but one whose justice would, it seems to me, be difficult to deny. Whether it is worth whatever reduction in national income that would result is a matter for 'pluralist' balancing of advantages but it would not be a high price for a rich society to pay.

The second line of attack would be to create by legislation an agency with power to tighten up incrementally the working conditions, material and psychological, that must be provided by any job and close down employers who fail to comply by certain deadlines. This would be a logical counterpart to other current moves to control the ill-effects of production more effectively. These ill-effects can be divided into three kinds. First, the process of production may damage the environment; second, the products may be dangerous or cause pollution (outstanding examples being cars and drugs); and, third, the process of production may be bad for the producers themselves. Each of these has a body of regulations governing it and an inspectorate which is supposed to enforce them. But the increased concern in the last few years with the first two, which has led to some small progress, scarcely seems yet to have touched the third.

The invariable trouble with regulatory agencies is the danger of their becoming too sympathetic with those they are supposed to control.[5] What is needed, I suggest, is the creation of a negative points system for the monotony, unpleasantness and danger of jobs, and legislation providing for the automatic reduction each year in the number of points a job can score and still be permitted to exist. In the advanced industrial societies few lines of reform, I suggest, hold a greater prospect for the advancement of human well-being.

5. This is a familiar enough story in relation to U.S. regulatory commissions. For a British example see Jeremy Bugler, *Polluting Britain* (Harmondsworth: Penguin, 1972), especially for the quotations from annual reports issued by the Alkali Inspectorate.

16

EPILOGUE

IN this book I have tried to keep Rawls's book, *A Theory of Justice*, in view all the time, and to follow wherever it led. I have now completed that task and I do not intend to waste time by recapitulating. What follows here is not, strictly speaking, part of the book but more a commentary on it. I have often found that off-the-cuff comments which people make are more useful in providing a key to their books than anything in it. For what they are worth, I am offering my own comments in print. They should be taken as conversational gambits rather than as a fully-armoured scholarly 'position'.

As I see it, then, the significance of *A Theory of Justice* is as a statement of liberalism which isolates its crucial features by making private property in the means of production, distribution and exchange a contingent matter rather than an essential part of the doctrine and introduces a principle of distribution which could, suitably interpreted and with certain factual assumptions, have egalitarian implications. If socialism is identified with public ownership or with equality, then this form of liberalism is compatible with socialism; though, by the same token, socialism defined on either of these criteria is also compatible with the antithesis of liberalism. The essence of liberalism as I am defining it here is the vision of society as made up of independent, autonomous units who co-operate only when the terms of co-operation are such as make it further the ends of each of the parties. Market relations are the paradigm of such co-operation, and this is well captured in the notion that the change from feudalism to the liberal apogee of the mid-nineteenth century was one 'from status to contract', and that subsequent developments reversed the process once again. Contract provides the model even for unpromising relationships such as political ones, where laws benefit some at the expense of others. The system as a whole is said to be beneficial to all, so everyone would agree in advance to its existence. As we have seen, Rawls presses this to its logical limit by deriving the principles of justice themselves from a notional 'social contract'.

Without, I hope, making it too obtrusive, I have had in mind throughout two alternative models of society to the liberal one, with which it can be compared. One is the hierarchical model, the other that of altruistic collaboration. As pure models of social co-ordination these three, I think, exhaust the possibilities. To reduce it to dyadic terms, A will do what B wants (i) because B has authority over A (hierarchy), (ii) because B makes it worth A's while to do it (liberalism) or (iii) because A wants to help B (altruistic collaboration). As the standard-bearer of the hierarchical model I chose Dr. Johnson. Boswell, in the 'Advertisement to the Second Edition' of his *Life*, puts the case for doing so: 'His strong, clear, and animated enforcement of religion, morality, loyalty, and subordination, while it delights and improves the wise and good, will, I trust, prove an effectual antidote to that detestable sophistry which has been lately imported from France, under the false name of *Philosophy* . . .'[1] I also used as an illustration Dostoyevsky's 'Grand Inquisitor', which was intended as an anti-socialist parable: 'our socialists (and they are not only the hole-and-corner nihilists) are conscious Jesuits and liars who do not admit that their ideal is the ideal of the coercion of the human conscience and the reduction of mankind to the level of cattle.'[2] As a diagnosis of the potential of Russian socialism this must be admitted to be remarkably accurate. The system of hierarchy could hardly be carried further than it was under Stalin: a divine figure of authority, a sacred body of orthodoxy (constantly amended) and death, quick or protracted, the penalty for heresy or insubordination. The model of altruistic collaboration I have not in the body of the book attributed to particular authors. In its most unlimited form it underlies the ideas of self-styled anarchists such as Godwin and Kropotkin, but I should prefer to mention, as a more sane line of development, that in English

---

1. Boswell, *Life of Johnson*, p. 7.
2. Letter quoted by David Magarshack in his Introduction to *The Brothers Karamazov*.

socialism running from William Morris's *News from Nowhere*, through R. H. Tawney's *The Acquisitive Society* to R. M. Titmuss's *The Gift Relationship*.[3] To these men socialism is not about distribution but human relationships—the right distribution is necessary to and made possible by the right relationships but it is morally of subordinate importance.

Any society is bound to be a mixture of the three models, and most people will find room in their own thinking for all of them, though different people will give them different priorities. It will have required no great detective-work to discover my own: I feel a strong attachment to liberalism in relation to ideas while believing that in matters of political, social and economic organization altruistic collaboration is worth giving up a good deal of efficiency for, and fearing that hierarchy is more soundly based in human psychology than I would altogether like.

3. London: Allen and Unwin, 1970.

LIST OF PASSAGES CITED

This list includes, arranged by sections of *A Theory of Justice*, the page number in this book of every quotation from Rawls amounting to more than two or three words, and also a few page numbers of places where a specific argument or passage is stated or summarized without direct quotation and the source given in the form '(See page . . .)'.

A Theory of Justice was published by the Belknap Press of Harvard University Press, Cambridge, Massachusetts, and by the Clarendon Press, Oxford, in 1972.